Cambridge El

Elements in Shakespeare

edited by
W. B. Worthen
Barnard College

SHAKESPEAREAN FUTURES

Casting the Bodies of Tomorrow on Shakespeare's Stages Today

Amy Cook
Stony Brook University

CAMBRIDGE
UNIVERSITY PRESS

CAMBRIDGE
UNIVERSITY PRESS

University Printing House, Cambridge CB2 8BS, United Kingdom

One Liberty Plaza, 20th Floor, New York, NY 10006, USA

477 Williamstown Road, Port Melbourne, VIC 3207, Australia

314–321, 3rd Floor, Plot 3, Splendor Forum, Jasola District Centre,
New Delhi – 110025, India

79 Anson Road, #06–04/06, Singapore 079906

Cambridge University Press is part of the University of Cambridge.

It furthers the University's mission by disseminating knowledge in the pursuit of
education, learning, and research at the highest international levels of excellence.

www.cambridge.org
Information on this title: www.cambridge.org/9781108749558
DOI: 10.1017/9781108782951

First published 2020

A catalogue record for this publication is available from the British Library.

ISBN 978-1-108-74955-8 Paperback
ISSN 2516-0117 (online)
ISSN 2516-0109 (print)

Shakespearean Futures

Casting the Bodies of Tomorrow on Shakespeare's Stages Today

Elements in Shakespeare Performance

DOI: 10.1017/9781108782951
First published online: October 2020

Amy Cook

Stony Brook University

Author for correspondence: Amy Cook, amy.cook@stonybrook.edu

ABSTRACT: Casting is the process by which directors assign parts to actors, creating the idea of the character for the audience. Casting is how we rehearse change, as we come to see an expanded repertoire of the kinds of bodies that are selected to play the lead, the hero, and the villain. This Element focuses on the casting in productions of Shakespeare from 2017 to 2020, demonstrating how casting functions affectively and cognitively to reimagine who can be what. The central argument is that directors are using casting as the central mode of meaning making in productions of Shakespeare.

KEYWORDS: Shakespeare, casting, cognitive, race, gender

ISBNs: 9781108749558 (PB), 9781108782951 (OC)
ISSNs: 2516-0117 (online), 2516-0109 (print),

Contents

1 Building Character

Alfred Hitchcock said that 75 percent of directing was casting. What he meant was that if the director gets the right actors in place, the majority of the storytelling work is done. Imagine, for example, if instead of casting Anthony Perkins in *Psycho* (1960) and James Stewart in *Rear Window* (1954), he reversed them. Both actors were white men of a certain age and both were clearly talented enough to be cast by Hitchcock. Stewart, however, as Norman Bates might have evoked George Bailey from *It's A Wonderful Life* (1946) for viewers, making him less mysterious and threatening. Just what does it mean to find the right actors and how do you know what makes one right and the other wrong? Casting, I argue, is not about mimesis or talent – though they may play a role in the decision; it's about creating a character at the intersection of the stimuli that get linked together when this actor walks on to play this role. Norman Bates is an idea; Perkins as Bates is a character.

Casting is how we build characters – this body, this actor, this text, this story, right now. Casting is how spectators can tell the difference between, say, Hamlet and Horatio. Making sense of the plot in a Shakespeare play can be difficult for audiences viewing contemporary productions; casting – particularly when directors cast celebrities – allows for spectators to quickly and efficiently accomplish the cognitive task of building a character where Ruth Negga and the text of *Hamlet* meet. What we know about the celebrity will help us anticipate the story we will see. Based upon what I know about Benedict Cumberbatch or Mel Gibson or Ruth Negga, I will expect a different production of *Hamlet*. Of course, spectators at Shakespeare's Globe had expectations for the character to be played by Richard Burbage or Robert Armin, too. But in a production of Shakespeare for contemporary audiences, casting is even more important, as most spectators do not bring to the story the same kind of character and story familiarity as an early modern audience would. Today, spectators may not walk into the theater with a wealth of information about Henry V or predictions about Malvolio based on his name, but when they know that Henry V will be played by Tom Hiddleston and Malvolio will be played by, say, David Hyde Pierce, they have a scaffold on which to make sense of the story.

Directors use casting to comment on the plays and the world surrounding the production; casting is never politically or ideologically neutral, as Claire Syler reminds us (Syler, 2019: 3). While this has always been true to an extent, I will focus on the casting in productions of Shakespeare from 2017 to 2020 to demonstrate how casting functions to move us to see things differently, to literally change our minds about who can be what and what can be. An actor walks onstage to play Beatrice, for example, in *Much Ado about Nothing* and, even before she opens her mouth, we are making judgments about what kind of Beatrice this is, what kind of love story, based on the actor. We may wonder to what extent the actor's race or gender or body type will be relevant (and in what way), but we see it. Directors can use casting to reflect the world we live in – so there will be a variety of different kinds of bodies onstage, just like in most of our lives. Or the director can cast a body counter to our expectations in such a way that we are invited to challenge our categories for ruler, lover, villain. I will discuss what I call *counter casting*, where bodies are used by the director against type to change our minds, to stretch and alter our categories. In productions of Shakespeare today, the casting of the actors is like the design revolution of Robert Edmond Jones a hundred years ago:[1] directors are using the bodies of the actors to tell us how we are to understand this old story now. I will examine the casting and staging of key contemporary productions of Shakespeare to argue that through these counter castings we can see the future we are grappling with, a future that's paradoxically hyper-attentive to the body while destabilizing the categories of race/ethnicity, gender, and even the idea of the self. These productions of Shakespeare are using casting to tell the future.

The future we are being shown, I believe, is one where the ecosystem and the group matter more than the individual. Hamlet's question about how the actor could feel for Hecuba remains crucial: How and why do we access real emotions about fictional people? Humans are really good at running scenarios about future events; we can imagine what will happen if

---

[1] Robert Edmond Jones is credited with integrating conceptual ideas of the play into the production design. Prior to this, the set might be practical or aesthetic, but it was not thought to contain thematic or artistic meaning.

the toddler follows the ball into the busy street or if we finally get that big promotion. It turns out, though, that we are not very good about predicting how we will feel in those situations. According to studies by psychologists Daniel T. Gilbert and Timothy D. Wilson, people tend "to overestimate the initial impact and/or duration of an emotional event" (Wilson & Gilbert 2013, 740). We think we will be happier and for a longer time if, say, our team wins the big game. Gilbert and Wilson suggest this hinders our ability to make smart decisions because we fail to accurately match past emotional experiences with potential future experiences and we think pleasure and pain will be greater than they actually are. Although thinking and feeling are often separated – as if one can think "clearly" without emotions or that emotions can "cloud" our thinking – they are inseparable. Our thinking about the future – our ability to see the trajectory of climate change or the future of democracy – evokes and requires feelings. Theater gives us a place to feel and imagine what the future might look; it allows us to live in the future. The future that directors are putting on stages today give us practice feeling the joy, the discomfort, the pathos, the surprise, of different bodies telling stories differently. These experiences might allow us to titrate our vision, our reactions, to the future because we have experiences that match. We are facing a future of ecological and social change; to face it, we need to change our metaphors and recast ourselves, our allies, and our stories.

Sometimes you have to go back to move forward.

1.1 Some Groundwork: Casting Is a Cognitive Process

Casting is a creative task of a director, but I also use the term to think about the process by which each of us organize and schematize information about the people on stage and all around us. The man in the coat becomes the doctor, the woman with the ruler becomes the teacher, and once these individuals are categorized – cast in a role – we can quickly make sense of how to interact with them.[2] Casting involves a process of compression,

---

[2] For a thorough discussion of the research in cognitive science that I draw on to make this argument, I refer the reader to *Building Character*. I argue there that casting is the process of creating characters at the intersection of stimuli and that it

efficiency, power, and complexity that is similar to the cognitive process involved in face recognition and our ability to look at a map and understand it as standing in for the place we are trying to navigate. How a play or film is cast shapes the thinking that is possible with and through that story in the same way that the degree to which we recognize a person's face influences the behavior called for by an interaction with that face. I'm fascinated by how we create characters and how we work through fiction to make sense of what we don't yet understand. My larger claim is that casting is part of how we stage who we are and who we can be. I talk about casting as a cognitive process – a way of categorizing and responding to the world around us – and I integrate theories of embodied and distributed cognition to make sense of how we process bodies in performance.

To suggest that casting is a cognitive process and that it is affectively and cognitively powerful is not to suggest that it is complicated, time-consuming, or specialized. The popularity of memes provides an excellent example of my meaning here. The "distracted boyfriend meme," wherein a man walking with his girlfriend is ogling another woman walking in the other direction, takes an instantly recognizable scenario with three clear characters and allows users to "cast" others into the role of the ogling boyfriend or a possible new girl. It's not necessary to "cast" people in these roles; in one version I saw, the boyfriend was labeled "me" and the girlfriend was labeled "productivity." The meme made it into the *New York Times* because it so quickly and efficiently was able to communicate what was going on between three car companies. On the front page of the business section on May 29, 2019, the *Times* illustrated their story about the imminent merger between Fiat Chrysler and Renault by casting the distracted boyfriend as Renault, the girlfriend upset at his ogling as Nissan, and the girl he's ogling as Fiat Chrysler. Without reading the article, I can guess what's going on by how

---

functions as a cognitive shorthand: "Though done most visibly by casting directors, all of us create characters by connecting bodies with roles. Characters, then, are a by-product of a cognitive system that can cast people. In this way, all characters are fictional" (Cook, 2018, 32). Here I will intentionally limit the theoretical scaffolding in order to focus on the performances under discussion.

the *Times* had cast these companies as the characters. Here's what the *Times* says in the article about the merger:

> If Jean-Dominique Senard, the chairman of Renault, can hold together the alliance while also merging with Fiat Chrysler, the combined entity would dominate the planet. . . . [Hiroto Saikawa, Nissan's chief executive] reacted warily to the proposed merger with Fiat Chrysler, which he learned about only days before it was announced. . . . Mr. Saikawa said that the merger could ultimately be beneficial, but that he needed "to closely examine it from Nissan's perspective." (Jack Ewing, Neal E. Boudette, & Ben Dooley, 2019: B1)

The car makers' situation both is and is not like the distracted boyfriend picture, but what the casting in the meme does successfully communicate is important enough to override the potential confusion it might bring to readers.

Readers did not think that Renault and Nissan had become boyfriend and girlfriend or that they were human or that one was male and the other female. On the other hand, where the text explains that Renault is hoping to have a relationship with Fiat Chrysler while maintaining its relationship with Nissan, that information is decidedly not in the meme. The meme suggests that the boyfriend might leave the girlfriend for the other but does not suggest that there's a possibility of his having both at the same time. This doesn't confuse readers either. The meme works because it swiftly communicates an emotional story on top of a business arrangement. It insists that the problem with the proposed merger is the likely emotional reaction Nissan might have to Renault's new merger. The meme also casts Renault's interest in physical and emotional terms: Renault as the "distracted boyfriend" turns, unable to stop itself, to look at an alternate possible future. To make sense of all this requires a complicated network of conceptual associations as well as emotions. Seeing our cognitive work in processing this meme allows us to understand how casting can be a tool to think with: tell me who plays the boyfriend, the girlfriend, and the ogled woman, and I will make new sense of a novel situation. Once I've learned the game, I can adapt it and use it for other things. Casting can be a powerful cognitive tool.

A performance speaks to us not just through our physical and emotional experience as an audience but also how we are "staged" or "cast" as spectators. As Evelyn Tribble brilliantly argues in *Cognition in the Globe* (2011) and Bruce Smith argues in *The Acoustic World of Early Modern England* (1999), the environment is critical to our thinking. This is usually called *distributed cognition*, and it is the theory that what we call "thinking" is a process that is spread out over the environment we are in. As Edwin Hutchins famously articulated in his *Cognition in the Wild* (1995), navigating a ship is a cognitive event that happens at the intersection of the captain, the crew, the layout of the control panel, and the ocean. Tribble points out that the cognitive feat of early modern actors being able to perform a rotating series of plays without much (or any) rehearsal is not due to the brilliance of the individuals, but of the system they are in, a system that includes the plots, the iambic pentameter, the props, the practice of acting apprenticeship, and the conventions of staging. When Richard Wagner designed Bayreuth with its hidden orchestra and fanned-out seats, he was affording his audience an experience of performance that was different from the one had in theaters created to facilitate spectators' views of each other. The small, intimate black-box theaters of the mid-twentieth century, on the other hand, were built to ensure focus on the faces of the actors in order to perceive the characters' "internal psychology." When actors in today's Shakespeare's Globe Theatre use the groundlings as confidants, rubes, foils, and props, the spectators understand the play in relation to this experience of being brought in on the joke. This isn't how all Shakespeare productions cast the audience, however, despite the ways that the scripts presume such a setting, but many contemporary productions of Shakespeare explicitly and critically cast the audience in a way central to the thematic content.

Recent theatrical experiences have required spectators to engage with the environment – not to make meaning but in order for us to enact an experience. Campbell Edinborough's book *Theatrical Reality* seriously considers the embodied spectator, embedded in space, and the role she plays in constructing the theatrical experience. Many of the performances he discusses rely on a staging, a placing, of the spectator into the experience.

This kind of performance puts the spectator into the scenic reality and strains and stretches the conventions of performer, author, and spectator. Edinborough analyzes an experience he had at a performance wherein a character reached out to hold his hand, and he suddenly felt himself both in and out of the drama: "As the actress held my hand, I wondered who I was supposed to be, which made me wonder who her character thought I was" (2016: 127). This "corporeal alienation" made it difficult for him to distinguish between theatrical reality and his own reality. What Edinborough does not discuss (but is my interest here) is what the cognitive/conceptual work of theatrical productions might be that stages the audience differently. If I am brought to my seat by an usher and told to turn my phone off and unwrap my candy and sit quietly in the dark when the play begins, I have been staged as part of the performance. My role has been cast: "Sit here; watch there." I may, like Claudius in *Hamlet*, imagine a relationship between what's on stage and my own life ("I also killed my brother"), but the two are separated by distance, darkness, and the "fourth wall." When theater companies disrupt this reception relationship, spectators need to challenge their interpretive protocols.

To be "cast" as a spectator may mean actually being given a role, as spectators were for Phyllida Lloyd's trilogy of all-female Shakespeare set in prison. Originally for the Donmar Warehouse in London, Lloyds' productions came to St. Ann's Warehouse in New York City.[3] In *Julius Caesar* (2012), *Henry IV*, *Part 1* (2014), and *The Tempest* (2016), the audience was marched into the "prison" under guard. Lloyd used the impact of the gates, the yelling, the dehumanizing cattle prodding of the entry to *Julius Caesar* to start the play by evoking the experience of threat, of restriction, of oppression. During the assassination, we are made to feel the threat of the conspirators from Caesar's perspective because the actor playing Caesar (Frances Barber) took the seat of an audience member in the front row. He is one of us, and we may be as vulnerable as he is. As Laura Seymour points out, this invites us to see and question our perspective:

---

[3] More information and clips from the productions are available here: https:// shakespeare-trilogy.donmarwarehouse.com/ The entire trilogy is available for free for teachers and students at UK schools.

> Occasionally turning round to address her lines to audience-members in a manner that suggested she expected sympathy and support from them, Barber consolidated this relationship and identification between Caesar and the audience. Simultaneously, via a camera trained on Barber's face, an image of Caesar's threatening countenance was shown on television screens positioned high up on either side of the stage. Thus, as well as experiencing Caesar's viewpoint of the conspirators as they knelt and looked up at him, the spectators could see Caesar's face looking down on them, as if they were in the conspirators' position. (Seymour, 2016: 51)

Playing the part of fellow prisoners, the spectators are invited to think about their perspective in their interpretations of the killing. With our attention drawn to our perspective – by shifting it, documenting it, challenging it – we wonder whose side are we on. Should Caesar have been killed? What is the environment, the situation, in which such a killing is necessary or inevitable?

Contemporary productions of Shakespeare sometimes cast spectators not by giving them a role within the play but rather a set of physical conditions through which to watch it. If, as philosopher Evan Thompson explains, the mind is "an embodied dynamic system in the world," not a "neural network in the head," our world is one we are trained to interact with in order to understand. Our environment is not background information; it is central to cognition. That is to say, according to Thompson, that "cognition unfolds as the continuous coevolution of acting, perceiving, imagining, feeling, and thinking" (Thompson, 2007: 10–11). This is the experience I had watching dreamthinkspeak's *The Rest Is Silence* in London in 2012. Staged in an empty warehouse space with the audience free to move about, watching scenes unfold in large window-spaces on the four walls around us, *The Rest Is Silence* connected my physical experience of navigating the story-consuming process with the nature of the story they were trying to tell. Flowing through the audience space, composing the story of *Hamlet* from the compressed and extended and overlapping scenes, I experienced the dispersion of cause, effect, agents, and intention; I was plugged into the network of beings that make up this cognitive event. *Hamlet* happens in the spectators' movement, in the rehearsal and performance of found text, in the shifting of perspectives, and in the redesignation of space.[4] In this case, performing the role of the audience meant moving and making choices with and through my body. I was cast to experience the play via my role as roving spectator – that was necessary to make sense of the production. Understanding cognition as embodied shifts what we can see and the questions we ask.

1.2 The Bodies in Shakespeare: Bodies Matter

The "casting director" is a very recent invention; Shakespeare did not cast his plays so much as write them for the bodies he had. As others have pointed out, his "clown" characters changed in 1599, when Will Kempe left the company and Robert Armin joined the company.[5] Writing *Hamlet* for Lord Chamberlain's Men meant writing Hamlet for Richard Burbage. Shakespeare's casting reality changed his text; as Paul Menzer reminds us, "Rosalind is not tall because the texts says so, the text says so because Rosalind is tall – at least the boy playing her was" (Menzer, 2013: 143). Shakespeare knew the actors, knew what they were capable of, what they had played before, and what the audience would anticipate about the story through reference to the actor. When Kemp entered as Dogberry in Act three of *Much Ado*, the audience would not need to wait until something funny happened to know it would be funny. Editor Harold Jenkins (1982) notes in the Arden *Hamlet* that the original actors of Hamlet and Polonius probably played Brutus and Caesar in the 1599 production of *Julius Caesar*, so when Burbage's Hamlet interacted with the Polonius that was his Caesar, audiences might have seen two plays at the same time, in a kind of character palimpsest. Shakespeare did not need to call attention to this, but he did, having Hamlet ask Polonius about his acting past before the Mousetrap. Polonius reports, "I did enact Julius Caesar. I was killed i'th' Capitol. Brutus killed me," and Hamlet responds, "It was a brute part of him to kill so capital a calf there" (3.2.101–4). In a kind of intertextual apology and/or

---

[4] For more on this performance, see Cook (2015).

[5] See, for example, Tiffany Stern (2004: 26).

ribbing, Hamlet/Brutus and Polonius/Caesar are all onstage together because the bodies cast to play the characters are made visible (to some) in the intertextuality.

The plays also often display the actors' bodies underneath the characters. In the badinage before the Mousetrap, Shakespeare provides a couple of metatheatrical moments to point out the actors playing Shakespeare's characters. After trading swipes with Claudius, Hamlet turns on Ophelia to suggest that he might lie in her lap. When she says no, Hamlet attempts to spin his request as nonsexual, but then says, "Do you think I meant country matters?" Primed by the discussion of her lap, an Elizabethan audience would hear the slang term for female genitalia in the first syllable of "country." Perhaps trying to change the conversation, which is occurring in front of the king, from the topic of her genitals, Ophelia says, "I think nothing, my lord," to which Hamlet replies, "That's a fair thought to lie between maids' legs"; when Ophelia falls for it and asks, "What is, my lord?," Hamlet replies, "Nothing" (3.2.116–21). This nothing, the lack of a penis thing, that lies between maids' legs, completes Shakespeare's peekaboo, undressing poor Ophelia. Played by a boy player, of course, Ophelia does have something between her legs and the audience gets to imaginatively "see" the missing thing of the character together with the thing of the actor.[6]

Though critics disagree about the degree to which audiences "forgot" they were watching boys play women, I find it far more interesting to imagine it fluidly, that sometimes the character had nothing between his or her legs and then at other times he had something. Anthony Dawson notes that a spectator writing about a male Desdemona wrote about the brilliance of the acting in which "she" seemed to "implore" in death. This critic is watching both: a dead female character and a male actor seeming to implore while pretending to be dead (Dawson, 1996; 35). Carol Chillington Rutter believes it was an "unremarkable" stage convention:

> The English stage didn't 'take' boys for women any more
> than it "took" commoners for aristocrats or Richard

---

[6] For more on this, see Cook, 2006.

> Burbage for Henry V. It did "take" players for the parts they
> played: that is, Elizabethan spectators, understanding actors
> as professionals whose business was role play, read the role
> played, not the player beneath the role. . . . I read Cordelia as
> "she", not "he." (Rutter, 2001: xiv)

She may "read" Cordelia as "she," but that's different from not noticing the
non-she-ness of Cordelia when played by a boy. Marjorie Garber is interested in the "relationship between cross-dressing and theatricality; the ways
in which clothing constructs (and deconstructs) gender and gender differ-
ences" (Garber, 1992: 3). For Garber, the boy player is a transvestite,
a figure of terror and seduction – a "monster of bothe kindes half women,
have men," as Stubbes says in *Anatomy of Abuses* (quoted in Garber, 1992:
36) – and thus "s/he incarnates and emblematizes the disruptive element
that intervenes, signaling not just another category crisis, but – much more
disquietingly – a crisis of 'category' itself" (Garber, 1992: 32). Phyllis
Rackin argues that the topic of gender was often-enough taken up in the
content of the plays – as well as in the convention of the boy player – that it
suggests that the theater provided a mechanism through which the early
modern audience could think about gender: "[T]heater provided an arena
where changing gender definitions could be displayed, deplored, or
enforced and where anxieties about them could be expressed by playwrights
and incited or repressed among their audiences" (Rackin, 1987: 39). It is the
very visibility of the actors' bodies that makes this play and display possible;
Ophelia's sex might be completely "unremarkable" up until the moment
the character's "nothing" is made the subject of Hamlet's joking before the
Mousetrap.

Shakespeare's periodic game of peekaboo suggests the bodies of the
actors were always available for staging, for taking advantage of to further
the story. Marvin Carlson (2001) calls this peekaboo "ghosting," arguing
that roles previously played by actors onstage can bleed through their
current characters. To be ghosted by a previous role can either enrich or
undermine a performance. A particularly unfortunate case of "ghosting" is
that of Kelsey Grammer as Macbeth on Broadway. According to Carlson,
the *New York Times* review of the production was centrally concerned with

the collision between Grammer's more famous character, Frasier Crane, and the title character of *Macbeth*. Reviewer Ben Brantley explains that Macbeth enters with vizard down at the start of the play to "forestall that disruptive shock of recognition that might prompt some rowdy theatre goer to yell out 'Where's Niles?' in reference to Frasier's television brother" (quoted in Carlson, 2001: 9). The ghost of Grammer's Frasier interfered in the reception of his Macbeth. Ghosting works effectively, on the other hand, when Kenneth Branagh casts Charlton Heston – an American actor known for over-acting – as the Player King in his *Hamlet* (1996).

Engaging with characters means bringing them to life, building them through a cognitive mechanism that Dan Rebellato likens to metaphor:

> I want to suggest that "David Tennant is Hamlet" in much the same way that love is a battlefield and all the world's a stage. In other words, David Tennant is a metaphor for Hamlet. In metaphor, we are invited to see (or think about) one thing in terms of another thing. There is no make-believe involved, no amassing of propositional information, no artful subtraction from one to create the image of the other. We know the two objects are quite separate, but we think of one in terms of the other. My suggestion is that this is precisely (not metaphorically) what happens in theatrical representation: when we see a piece of theatre we are invited to think of the fictional world through this particular representation. Theatrical representation is metaphorical. (Rebelatto, 2009: 25)

I agree that we can simultaneously know that the two are separate and also see one in terms of the other, but I would argue that the connection doesn't just go one way. Sometimes we think of Hamlet through David Tennant and sometimes we think of David Tennant through Hamlet. The two ideas become connected, and where they come together, there is a possible new world – a world in which David Tennant is Hamlet and Hamlet is David Tennant. Perhaps for some viewers, familiar with Tennant as Doctor Who, this is a Hamlet who is partially Doctor Who. Think about Kenneth Branagh's turn as Hamlet: staging his first appearance with his bleached blond hair to immediately echo Lawrence Olivier's *Hamlet* (1948), it was clear that Branagh wanted to evoke a lineage of actors changed by Hamlet and Hamlets changed by the actors who played him. Or, more visibly, consider the powerful and sometimes questionable ways in which the historical Alexander Hamilton has been changed through Lin-Manuel Miranda.[7]

Casting that invites or demands a shifting of categories, I call counter casting. This is not just "blind" or "nontraditional"; it's closer to what Brandi Wilkins Catanese calls "nonconforming casting" (Catanese, 2011, 18). It shares elements with Faedra Chatard Carpenter's important analysis of Dave Chappelle's "nonconforming whiteness" sketches – performances that deploy bad make-up to create an "incomplete optic whiteface" that then "alludes to the fact that those among us who may represent whiteness are, indeed, not really white at all but rather are – consciously or unconsciously – passing as such" (Carpenter, 2014; 185). Counter casting is casting that calls attention to itself; its casting the "wrong" body in order to change the conversation and alter the story. It can be subtle or radical, but it is always political. It counters our thinking and offers a new story for the characters and ourselves. It is not like "plastic representation" discussed by Kristen Warner whereby non-white bodies are cast as white characters without changing the parts, "in order to flatten the expectation to desire anything more" (Warner 2017). Tamsin Greig was noteworthy as a female Malvolio in *Twelfth Night* at the National, but a female Malvolio did not change the story of the play. I am not sure what can be learned by an "age-blind" *Hamlet* starring Ian McKellen – other than some bodies think they belong everywhere – but I will reserve my judgment.[8] On the other hand, Lin-Manuel Miranda's *Hamilton* altered the story of the founding of America and also invited its spectators to expand their categories of what political leadership looks like.[9]

---

[7] For example, there's a T-shirt with the bust of Hamilton in sunglasses with the tagline "My favorite rapper is Alexander Hamilton."

[8] News of this production, directed by Sean Matthias, focused on the precautions needed for actors – particularly older actors – to return to rehearsal during the pandemic of 2020, so they are not "blind" to McKellen's age (eighty-one) in planning rehearsals.

[9] Although I agree, in part, with Galella's criticism that in *Hamilton*, "[t]he casting of people of color to embody typically white characters thus showcases the nation

Crucially, this does not mean that white people can suddenly take on roles meant for black or brown bodies and hope it will make a point and not just be stupid, offensive, or both. Casting white actors in parts meant for nonwhite actors can garner unwanted press and angry Twitter discussions and sometimes get your show closed. While it may be unwise to condemn all such casting as "whitewashing," it is clear that care must be taken in such instances. The old saw about the "best actor for the job" simply will not do. Bodies matter and so does context. Whenever I have talked about casting in an educational setting, someone asks me about whether or not a school should avoid plays if the casting can't match the identity of the character. This presents an opportunity for students and educators to have difficult conversations and to hone their critical-thinking skills. In response to this educational challenge—where strict rules about what bodies can tell what stories may go against the mission of the school and make storytelling limited, theater scholar Patricia Ybarra (2015) has called for "coalitional casting." Brian Herrera glossed Ybarra's term in his essay on the staging of Latinx plays on college campuses, where the student body may not match the called-for racial bodies of the play's characters:

> Coalitional casting does not rely upon the sloppy shorthand of racial mimicry, but instead deploys ethnic surrogation as a strategic means of underscoring the structural gaps that exist within the American theatre, especially those parts of the theatrical ecosystem like the university stage that are limited in how they can hire in ethnically analogous performers. . . . [A] coalitional approach instead insists on a principle of "ally-ship" to guide the work of performance,

as equal, diverse, and inclusive but only under the terms of emphasizing white history makers and softening the salience of race and racism" (Galella, 2018: 372), I maintain that the experience of *Hamilton* as a public, cultural event does challenge our categories of leaders. While it clearly fails to take on the racism of the past, in part through casting actors of color, it invites its audience to reimagine history into the future through a cast of brown and black bodies.

> leveraging privilege to amplify awareness of racial and
> ethnic inequity rather than efface it. (Herrera, 2017: 31–32)

This foregrounds the empathy involved in becoming another and allows for
the failure to fully represent the other to be upstaged by the beauty of the
storytelling possible when we try anyway. Ybarra calls this coalitional
casting because "being onstage in these roles is not only an act of becoming
a culturally different person, but an act of committing to the cause of telling
a marginalized story; it is committing to doing the work it takes to get over
one's trepidation over telling someone else's story. And it requires realizing
that no single story is universal unless everyone's story is" (Ybarra, 2015).
Watching a production of, say, *In The Heights* on a college campus, my
attention is brought to the work the cast has done to make sense of the
people they are traveling to – not because the representation is easy or
already authentic, but because it requires brave and rewarding *work* to
represent what you are not. Again, like the distinction between nontraditional casting and counter casting, the difference is in the work and care
made to call attention to the bodies and the always-incomplete travel from
actor to character.

1.3 Why Casting Now: Going Back to Move Forward

Actors have been playing Shakespeare's characters almost nonstop since
he wrote them, so why should there be particular attention to casting in
Shakespeare now? Celebrities have always operated as a way to communicate complicated story information to a modern audience by reducing the
cognitive load of keeping track of the many characters in the play. The
Masks Of series by Rosenberg (1961–2006) describes the history of actors
playing key roles but does not talk about the role of casting a particular
actor as a particular character. In Ralph Berry's 1989 book *On Directing
Shakespeare*, there's a lot of talk of décor/concept (Michael Kahn's terms),
historical placement, and cutting, but almost no discussion of casting. Right
now, I cannot imagine talking about *Much Ado about Nothing* in Central
Park without talking about casting. I could hardly say anything about
Michelle Terry's inaugural season as Artistic Director of Shakespeare's

Globe without referring to casting. I couldn't explain the difference between the five *King Lear*s that I have seen in the past two years without talking about casting. Casting is central to meaning making in productions of Shakespeare now, and I believe we can see this in how these directors return to the old in order to generate the new. King Lear as an idea is stable (if multiple); King Lear as a woman is a new vision of kingship. In addition to the obvious casting choices of a female Lear or an all African American *Much Ado about Nothing*, I want to explore the nuanced ways that directors are using casting to help spectators envision an identity of tomorrow.

The next three sections work toward a coherent argument about how casting is the prism through which Shakespearean directors are generating images of who we could be going forward. I will often gesture toward *Building Character* (2018), but this book operates separately as a record of performances from the last three to four years with particular attention to the bodies of the actors onstage. In the next section, I will talk about the race, gender, and (dis)ability in contemporary productions of Shakespeare, arguing that some bodies are more visible than others. From 2017 to 2019, there have been many high-profile productions of *King Lear*. From Ian McKellan in a National Theatre production and Anthony Sher in an RSC production in 2018, to Anthony Hopkins in an Amazon film (2019) and Glenda Jackson in a Broadway production (2019), Lear has been everywhere. I will explore these productions guided by an assumption that we stage what we do not understand. The final section will briefly look at the productions of the less visible, but influential, avant-garde theater companies like Pan Pan and Forced Entertainment. Given what we've seen in the past few years, where does it look like directors want to take us next?

Casting is how we rehearse change. What does it take to come to see an immigrant as a citizen, a woman as president, or a person as ungendered? From boy players to Mark Rylance, scholars have been interested in how casting has interrogated or challenged questions of gender. In the past fifty years, directors pointed to "non-traditional casting" to open up Shakespeare to nonwhite actors. There is a critical difference, however, between casting that is supposedly "blind" to race or gender and casting that specifically uses the bodies of the actors to respond to the play and to stage the future. Theater, like the arts in general, reflects current scientific truths: as Joseph

Roach (1993) showed in *The Player's Passion*, acting stages the scientific understanding of the playwright and actors. In addition to staging what is, casting might also stage what can be possible. Casting helps us understand meaning as something that is composed and thus as something we can compose differently. If characters are built, then they can be rebuilt; we need not be passive receivers of characters.

2 The Visible Body

Writing this in the summer of 2019, I could have chosen from any one of many examples of casting conversations happening in the news or on social media. Ali Stroker became the first actor in a wheelchair to win a Tony for Best Actress in a Musical for Ado Annie in *Oklahoma!* Halle Bailey was cast as the lead in *The Little Mermaid*. Lashana Lynch was set to become 007 – but not James Bond. Scarlett Johansson, angry that backlash forced her to withdraw from playing a transgender man in a movie called *Rub & Tug*, asserted, "You know, as an actor I should be allowed to play any person, or any tree, or any animal because that is my job and the requirements of my job" (Dry 2019). She was roundly ridiculed by Trevor Noah of *The Daily Show* (2019), among others. Bodies are making characters differently visible. As *Vox* put it in their coverage of the Johansson quote, "Philosophically, anyone should be able to play anyone, sure. But the truth is that Hollywood clearly doesn't subscribe to that idea on a broad basis; instead, it's white people who can seemingly play anyone" (Frank 2019). Noah's retort to Johansson's claim mostly focused on the politics of inclusion and the importance of representation, though he ended by warning against "stifling creativity in the arts" (2019). For Noah, the politics of the body are clear, though what is visible about the body is less clear; Johansson's body is not a Japanese robot or a trans man, but not all transsexuals or homosexuals are "out," Noah says, so that need not be a criterion. Casting is a critical part of meaning making in theater and film, even if it's not always given the kind of critical attention it deserves. As Brian Herrera has put it, "The assignment of this particular actor to that specific role is, quite often, an inceptive interpretive gesture – a mechanism for making performance happen, and a way to manifest meaning within performance. These two aspects of casting – making performance and manifesting meaning – readily become so twined as to appear as singular, even inevitable" (Herrera, 2019: 49). The critical project undertaken here is to demonstrate how much meaning is happening right now in productions of Shakespeare through the casting of new bodies as old characters.

Both onstage and off, the body is a visible and critical part of the actor and character. Scarlett Johansson's argument about being able to play any part will sound familiar: acting is about talent and a good actor should be able to play anyone. This self-centered formulation obscures the real question; sure, actors can *play* anyone, but spectators will see the actors' bodies as the characters' bodies. This, as I hope to show here, can lead to profoundly moving and radical performances (a deaf Celia, a female Lear) and also some troubling ones (a deaf Guildenstern, an African American Fool). Although this section will start with questions of race on the Shakespeare stage, there are many examples of visible bodies driving storytelling. Theater *is* bodies telling stories onstage, and what those bodies look like always has been a critical part of the larger story (if not also the micro-story) being told when that story takes the stage on that day and in that place. Although in many ways this whole project is about bodies made exceptionally visible through creative casting, I want to focus here on how race, gender, and ability are central to the stories that directors want to tell here and now. The headline for Matt Wolf's *New York Times* review of Michelle Terry's first season as Artistic Director of Shakespeare's Globe makes my point nicely: "Blind to Race, Gender and Disability, Shakespeare's Globe Goes a New Way" (Wolf 2018). Wolf's essay is all about the visibility of the casting – so visible, in fact, that Wolf fails to see Terry's "guiding directorial hand," which he feels is missing. Whatever the quality of her directing might be, her deliberate engagement with questions of race, gender, and ability in her casting choices makes her one of several powerful and important directors right now.

2.1 Race Onstage

When one does American work, it is often about race, because race is our underlining tragedy in this country. It's the wound that we are continually trying to heal. So a theatre that focuses on American work, it's always gonna be there. So in a profound way, I'm answering that through casting.

Molly Smith, Artistic Director of Arena Stage[10]

In a telling anecdote in *The Problem of the Color[blind]* (2011), Brandi Wilkins Catanese talks about playing Rosalind in class and coming upon the line about her "lily-white hand." Catanese's hands were not white, and no quality of acting was going to change that. Some in the audience might suggest this means that Catanese is poorly cast as Rosalind – that Rosalind is meant to be white. Some in the audience might notice the line but assume they were to be "blind" to the actor's race. Others might be reminded of just how white the Western canon is. Catanese reports following up this line with a look at her hands and a look to the audience as if to say, "I see what you see." This allows all of those reactions to remain open for the spectators: if we assume Rosalind was meant to be white, we might realize that it is nonetheless not a terribly salient element of her character in this performance, as evidenced by the fact that Catanese's gesture suggests that it hadn't been important to her before this moment. If we thought we were to ignore the line, we are now wondering why we would pretend not to notice when the actor herself is noticing. If we were irked by yet another performance of a white playwright's play about white people, we now see that the actor herself is not trying to "pass" but is rather making a skillful intervention. In this moment, with another character clearly describing the color of Rosalind's skin in a way that belies what all of us can see about the actor's skin, Catanese's body becomes hypervisible. How she chooses to deal with that moment is up to her and the director. Through her gesture, Catanese generates irony by opening up a distance between the character and the actor. Spectators must understand the story and the character by folding together Catanese's perspective on her hand as well as the author's perspective on Rosalind's hand. This layering adds complexity and richness and invites us to question our own perspective on race.

In addition to Catanese's wonderful book, one can turn to the work by Ayanna Thompson (2019, 2011, 2010, 2006), Angela Pao (2010), and Ania

---

[10] Quoted in Galella, 2015: 218.

Loomba (2006) on race and casting for rich historical and theoretical examinations of the topic. As Thompson tells us, reactions to "color-blind" casting in Shakespeare are often divided between people who tend to argue that race in the classics is not an issue because they are nonnaturalistic and therefore "universal" and those who argue that there is no such thing as a play freed from history. But "both sides assume that race does not always exist in performance. The universalist/non-naturalist argument assumes that whiteness is normative and, therefore, not raced. The cultural-specifist/naturalist argument is often so focused on actors of color that it neglects race in/as performance *in terms of whiteness itself*" (Thompson, 2011: 189). August Wilson famously argued that "[c]olorblind casting is an aberrant idea that has never had any validity other than as a tool of the Cultural Imperialists" (Brustein & Wilson, 1996).[11] Its ideological problem is also its artistic problem: it doesn't work. We are never blind to color; color-blind casting asks us to "erace" color and to pretend that it is not playing a part – a position that is a powerful tool of the white status quo. As Donatella Galella reminds us, "How we read bodies onstage mediates, and is mediated by, how we read them offstage" (Galella, 2018: 214). Shakespeare's perceived universality means not that we can be blind to color in casting but rather that we look to race to help us understand how this old story is being retold, anew, today. As Ania Loomba puts it, "to pay attention to colorblind casting of Shakespeare is to do nothing less than to engage in the most vital discussions about identity, performance, and the politics of contemporary multiculturalism" (Loomba, 2006: xvii). This we must do, and we must do it now.

To achieve this goal, we must recognize the relationship between casting and ideology as much as casting and "reality." The language of traditional conversations around race and casting focus on conventions of realism – a style that loves to rehearse racist and misogynistic structures as "natural" and "realistic." Ralph Berry divides the characters and types that can and cannot be played by nonwhite actors. His logic for why Adrian Lester as Hamlet works but a black Cordelia does not is strained: "*Hamlet* can be seen as a solo-part play, a concerto for soloist and (chamber) orchestra, so Peter

---

[11] Both authors respond here to Wilson's keynote address to the Theatre Communications Group's Conference of June 1996.

Brook's casting of Adrian Lester caused no great stir. After all, the aged Sarah Bernhardt had played Hamlet. Even so, a black Cordelia engages the mind in tortuous moves. (Did Lear re-marry? I knew a distinguished scholar who was convinced that Lear had three queens.)" (Berry, 2004: 36). What defines this concerto? Hamlet's paternity is even more relevant to the plot of Hamlet than Cordelia's is; why doesn't Lester's Hamlet engage the mind in tortuous moves? Hamlet has both of his parents onstage – as opposed to Cordelia, whose mother we never see – so there's no missing explanation. The fact that there is such an obvious answer, one that Berry himself provides, to a racial difference between the Lear daughters suggests it's not that tortuous.

Berry assumes that we build characters based on the controlling instructions of the text, genetics, and realism: the textual evidence of race is strong enough to require that Aaron and Othello at least seem "other," but Morocco, despite the same textual evidence, matters less because he "is such a lightweight that strong feelings will not be aroused by his casting" (Berry, 2004: 38). I understand that, for Berry, the size of the character of Morocco means that the identity marker of the actor doesn't matter as much to the story, but it's telling that he is concerned about feelings. For some characters, race is actually decidedly unimportant – like servant characters, who "arrive on stage without any burden of ethnic expectation" (Berry, 2004: 36). Berry seems to write for the feelings and expectations of a white audience and white actors. He seems to eschew realism when the feelings and expectations of white actors are at stake: "Cleopatra really should have a 'tawny front', but never does, mainly because white actresses have no intention of letting go their chances" (Berry, 2004: 38). Realism allows for the flexibility required by privilege and ideology; casting that privileges realism reinforces existing power structures by refusing to let us see them as something we can change. As Elin Diamond has argued in her Brechtian and feminist critique of realism, "Realism disgusted Brecht not only because it dissimulates its conventions but because it is hegemonic: by copying the surface details of the world it offers the illusion of lived experience, even as it marks off only one version of that experience" (Diamond 1988; 87). Casting that frustrates mimesis by countering the "surface details" challenges viewers to alter how they make sense of the characters built onstage.

The protocols for the reception of race onstage in Shakespeare are changing. Since Joseph Papp started "color-blind" casting at the Delacorte in 1962, audiences have seen bodies that did not match the presumed race or ethnicity of the characters represented, and this has led to an expectation that realism or mimesis will not (necessarily) control the casting. I do not believe, however, that color-blind casting is ideal or even possible. In 2013, Jami Rogers diagnosed "the State of Colorblind Casting in Contemporary British Theatre" as the "Shakespearean Glass Ceiling," arguing that productions seemed to be blind to race only in relation to the minor parts (Rogers, 2013: 406). What I want to make clear is that we (spectators and theater makers) must be *more* attentive to the value and the importance of the race, gender, sex, size, and ability of the actors we cast. We must practice building characters that may not look like they did yesterday but reflect what they resemble today and will resemble tomorrow. Skin color is not always the most salient part of the character; the text and other performance choices of the director can make it so that even though we see it, it's not relevant to our experience, so we move past it. This is particularly true in productions from the past few years: Casting in Shakespeare is expected to represent the racial diversity of the community and so critics rarely comment on the race of an actor playing Celia or Hamlet or Brutus. This is true even when the racial difference for the character brings up questions of genetics. In both Anthony Sher's and Ian McKellan's productions of *King Lear*, Cordelia is played by a black actress. In neither case did reviewers comment on this casting choice (despite her other two sisters being played by white actresses), nor did I think her skin color played a significant role in the experience of the play. This troubles me, though, as it feels like an erasure. With both Cordelias, I wanted to find meaning in their race: a nod to the growing importance of women of color in American politics, perhaps. This does not mean that we are now "color-blind" but rather that the convention of realism in Shakespearean representation has changed to an interest in the layering of stories through the building of complex characters.

These complex characters are built through casting. How this happens – particularly as it relates to race, gender, and ability – has generated tremendous interest in the last five years. In their 2019 edited volume *Casting a Movement: The Welcome Table Initiative*, Claire Syler and Daniel Banks include a timeline of critical moments in casting, starting with the initiation of "integrated casting" by Joseph Papp at the New York Shakespeare Festival. In her contribution to the book, Ayanna Thompson emphasizes the centrality of race and gender in the interpretation of performance:

> Take the example of Prospero from *The Tempest*. Theatrically, revenge looks really different when expressed by different bodies. *The Tempest* has different cultural valence if it is a White Prospero or a Black Prospero or Asian Prospero and taking into account the gender identity of the actor. . . . Because I never assume that one's body can be read in a color-blind fashion, I felt that I was constantly seeing a different play than my fellow audience members who seemed reluctant to admit that the race of the bodies onstage mattered. (Thompson, 2019: 34)

Bodies matter, and when spectators are trying to make sense of a complicated story or trying to keep track of a number of different characters, they offload some of the cognitive work to the bodies/faces of the actors. This is part of why celebrities are so popular onstage: They dramatically reduce the amount of cognitive work required to build a character because we come into the story knowing and anticipating who they will be based on who we have seen them to be. Casting can decrease complexity by complementing – or even upstaging – the information provided in the text with the body and history of the actor. Casting can also increase complexity, in a pleasurable way, when the actor does not fit the text and we must reimagine the story – and our politics – to make sense of the scene before us.

The scene before us is always understood given the world around us; casting is always historically contingent. This is clear in the story of two different productions of *Oklahoma!* Galella starts her analysis of the casting in the Arena Stage's 2010 "multiracial" production of *Oklahoma!* by saying, "Multiracial casting, and interpretations of that casting, raise high stakes for practitioners, academics, and audiences invested in social justice. How we read bodies onstage mediates, and is mediated by, how we read them offstage" (Galella, 2015: 214). Galella suggests three possible ways that such performances can be read: (1) a "multiracial utopia" where the races of the actors are staged to suggest a world where all bodies sing and dance together; (2) a cast that is "playing" white, thus whitewashing the bodies of the actors; and (3) a performance where "producers and spectators could, through sense-making of the cast in a present-day, allegedly post-racial, nonracist, colorblind world, perceive the cast and characters as transcending race, ultimately deeming race unimportant" (Galella, 2015: 216). Galella's interviews with the production team reveal the care and rigorous attention they paid to the ways the bodies would signify, debating the implications, for example, of a mixed-race Jud. This production, according to Galella, inspired its multiracial audience: "The affect of joy and hope provoked by witnessing and participating in multiracial harmony can, in turn, provoke actions that make that harmony a reality outside the theater" (Galella, 2015: 198). This third option was an option available to D.C. audiences in 2010 during the early years of the presidency of Barack Obama – "another black actor in a typically white role" (Galella, 2015: 210). However, this option was far less available for the spectators at Daniel Fish's production at St. Ann's Warehouse in 2018.

Fish's production also used multiracial casting but was understood within a different context. In the *New York Times*, Ben Brantley and Jesse Green discuss how the "stark illumination" and the "wall of shotguns" unveils a very dark America: "What's so thrilling about this exposure of what lies beneath is that you feel it was always there, waiting to be excavated" (Green & Brantly, 2018). This is precisely the feeling many Americans had facing the racism, sexism, and nationalism that seemed to come in reaction to Obama's presidency and this production felt in direct conversation with the Trump desire to Make America Great Again; this America wasn't all white and it wasn't all that great. The play ends with Curley shooting Jud, but the blood covers Curley and Laurey. As in the original musical, the town lets Curley off, but the blood will not leave them. This ending, for Green, fits: "[T]here was no way he [Fish] was going to leave us, in 2018, with an uncomplicated feeling about the workings of justice in America or about the wisdom of having formed a union from incompatible states" (Green & Brantly, 2018). Rebecca Naomi Jones, who is black, played Laurey and Mary Testa, who is white, played Aunt Eller. I suppose there might be spectators who insisted on coming up with some genetic explanation for their lack of familial resemblance, but I would argue that we perceive that choice in the context of other black and mixed-race cast members. In other words, Jones's race matters here, but not the way we might think. Her body is also complemented by the body of Gabrielle Hamilton who performs Laurey's (dramaturgically odd) dream ballet. This ballet, choreographed by John Heginbotham, presents Laurey's sexual desire as athletic and powerful. When Hamilton exits and Jones enters, we know what was expressed by Hamilton is felt by Jones. Ado Annie is played by Ali Stroker who, as Ben Brantley points out "turns her wheelchair into an all-conquering tool that matches her sly, vanquishing smile" (Green & Brantley, 2018). Stroker's wheelchair does not disappear and yet we do not think of Annie as disabled. It is unremarkable and unremarked on. Stroker is so powerful, so able, that we do not change our idea of Annie, we change our idea about people in wheelchairs. In 2018, we read the bodies differently, but we still read them within a political context.

In the Public Theater's 2019 *Much Ado about Nothing*, all the roles were played by black actors. In an interview, director Kenny Leon said that he began "building" his idea of the play around Danielle Brooks as Beatrice. In speaking about how this Beatrice is different, both director and actor referred to both her color and her size. Brooks said, "I was sold because a role like Beatrice doesn't come around often for someone like me, a black, plus size woman. It felt bigger than myself." And Leon said, "She's a beautiful, talented, plus size advocate and I wanted to create a Beatrice no one had ever seen before" (Giannotta, 2019). Once she was secured as his Beatrice, he decided to place it in Atlanta during the 2020 election because he wanted it to reflect the America he wanted now and hoped he would have in the future: "I wanted to set it in a community that was embracing those values we stand for in America: gender equality, racial equality and the fact that love always wins" (Giannotta, 2019). Having the first all-black cast at the Delacorte Theatre did not drive his creative vision from the start, perhaps, but the impact of the all-black cast on the story and experience of the play was great.

In his review for the *New York Times*, Jesse Green said, "They [Brooks and Grantham Coleman, who plays Benedict] and the rest of the cast are black – and not in a colorblind-casting way, which would suggest they were pretending to be white" (Green, 2019). The show was generally sold out and was also filmed for the BBC, which gave it a successful television and now streaming run as well. What the audiences came to see was a story about today told by this community of actors through a play written four hundred years in the past set in an imagined future. Audiences knew it was 2020 America because of the large "Stacey Abrams 2020" sign on the set. We also knew that the director had "cast" our real-world political candidate for 2020 as a (plus size) black woman at the start of a play we knew was starring a plus-sized black woman. These bodies, we know, matter. Further, when Don Pedro and his men return from "battle," they carry signs that say things like "I Am a Person," signaling that today the battles we must fight are categorical. Who gets to love, and who gets to be believed?

Casting actors of different races and ethnicities in roles traditionally presumed white is no longer always radical, but it does continue to push our categories and expand who we expect to see where. All of the productions of Shakespeare's plays that I have seen in the past three years have contained at least one nonwhite actor. Leon's production did use casting to, at least in part, retell the story, but many simply used a diverse cast to reflect a diverse community and the weakening of realism as a mode of character building. This is different from color-blind casting that pretends that the actor's race or color doesn't matter; instead, this approach to casing says that perhaps the original character's race doesn't matter. It's not that we don't notice that, for example, Orlando is black in the 2019 RSC production of *As You Like It*; it's that we don't care that he was ever anything else. Even in a play that refers to the white hand of Rosalind, we can see the actors' skin color without thinking there is a statement being made about it – unless, that is, the director calls our attention to the narrative possible with those bodies. Leon's production ends, after the singing and dancing, with the men leaving again in military formation with their signs; it's once again time to remind the world, again, that these bodies matter. Yet for a couple of hours, these very particularly raced and placed bodies still love, laugh, sing, and march.

2.2 Gender Onstage

Leon's production also handles Claudio's betrayal of Hero by giving her, as David Cote of *The Observer* noted, a small amount of "agency," allowing

Margaret Odette's Hero to rage and fight the unfair destruction of her good name (Cote, 2019). This Hero has been betrayed by men but will not necessarily spend her life a victim of them. In the sequel I played out in my mind, Hero runs for Congress buoyed by the #MeToo movement, and Claudio runs her campaign in the background. Nonetheless, the text does not supply that agency. As many have experienced, playing a female character in Shakespeare often requires justifying silence, or submission, or acceptance of the unacceptable. Rhonda Blair's (1985) essay on feminist performance articulates the mismatch between embodying Shakespeare's too-often-silent women. Actors can rage, or roll their eyes, or wink at the audience, but they cannot change the plays they are in. One university director swore he was going to direct a feminist *Taming of the Shrew*, and I laughed. The play works very powerfully against such a reading. As I argued in *Building Character* (2018), though, casting all women in the play can upend our protocols of perception around gender. Phyllida Lloyd's *Shrew* at The Public in 2016 balanced the hypergendered and patriarchal world by casting women to play all the parts. Gremio, played by Judy Gold, tells sexist jokes to the audience about the show she is trapped in: "You know this show is directed by a woman! They all have boobs!" When one audience member shouted out "Enough with the misogyny!," Gold shouted back, "You feminists have no sense of humor: we're all women, get it?" The presence of all female bodies on this stage is critical to the reception: no matter how butch or femme these characters seem, they all have boobs.

There is a convention of casting Petruchio and Kate with actors who are married in real life. Carlson (2001) doesn't address this kind of ghosting, when the off-screen relationship between the actors is relied upon to counter and comment on the onscreen/onstage relationship, but there are websites devoted to celebrity couples who have played couples on film. The complexity of the actors and the characters being married both in and out of the storyworld provides a rich layering of love, desire, betrayal, and a doubling that allows comparison: the storyworld marriage versus the real-world marriage. Casting a famously married couple in *Taming of the Shrew* became a "gimmick" for actors and directors after Oscar Asche and Lily Brayton first played Katherina and Petruchio in London in 1904. Alfred Lunt and Lynne Fontanne also brought their marriage onstage for

129 performances of *Taming of the Shrew* in 1930. Margaret Loftus Ranald suggests that the offstage marriage simultaneously softens the "apparent cruelty of the play," and can also lend "titillation to this play of matrimonial strife" (Ranald, 1994: 217). Two other notable twentieth-century *Shrew*s brought an offstage marriage onstage: Sam Taylor's 1929 version and Franco Zeffirelli's film of 1967. John Brett Mischo commented:

> No doubt the on-screen relationship between Pickford's Kate and Fairbanks' Petruchio played to the audiences and their awareness of the couple's well-publicized, often stormy marriage (as would Zeffirelli's version, almost forty years later, with Taylor and Burton). Present too, in the mind of the American audience, would have been the social upheaval of the recent women's suffrage movement and the passage in 1920 of the Nineteenth Amendment enfranchising women as voting citizens. (Mischo, 2002: 218)

No doubt. And many critics have analyzed the different ways that the two Kates respond to their "taming" in the final speech. Diana Henderson notes the play's "obsessive return to the screen – particularly during the decades of 'backlash' when advances in women's participation outside the home have prompted a response from those who perceive a threat" (Henderson, 2004: 149). What the spectators are being asked to examine, though, is not the women but the couples. The two films fantasize for their audiences two different kinds of marriages.

It wasn't just women who were changing during the twenties and sixties in America; it was the marriages they were in. In 1929, Mary Pickford was tamed by her off-screen husband, Douglas Fairbanks, and ended the speech with a wink at the camera. When Elizabeth Taylor and Richard Burton played the couple in 1967, Taylor ended it by yelling and running off, forcing her Petruchio to follow her. Although both marriages were fairly famously falling apart at the time, the story told by things like "Pickfair" and tabloid depictions of passion is one of the capacious potentials of marriage: you don't have to always agree in order to move forward and stay in the bond. Who wouldn't want to imagine being in the union of Lunt and Fontaine, Pickford and Fairbanks, or Taylor and Burton? The power of the offscreen relationship is such that the onscreen relationship is validated and romanticized simply because if that's what it looks like to be married to Liz Taylor, so be it. And the idea of marriage is strengthened by imagining a world in which Elizabeth Taylor lets Richard Burton do that to her. The offstage marriage makes the violence feel safe because it is consensual – a mutual desire – and thus a feature of the relationship, not a problem.[12] Whether you wink or run, these films are saying, there's no escaping the marriage bond.

Taylor and Burton also played George and Martha in *Who's Afraid of Virginia Woolf?* (1967), another damaged couple in a destructive marriage. Casting fictional married couples with actual married couples invites the spectators to see marriage as transcending the storyworld; no matter what happens on this two hour's traffic of the stage, these two will go home together. Perhaps having the real-life husband present allows the real-life wife to be a far more dangerous storyworld wife. In early 2020, *Medea* came to the Brooklyn Academy of Music. Written and directed by Simon Stone, this play about a difficult wife stars Bobby Cannevale and Rose Byrne, who are married in real life. Another famous couple was onstage in New York during the fall of 2019: "real life" husband and wife Corey Stoll and Nadia Bowers played Macbeth and Lady Macbeth. The press for both of these productions focuses on the offstage relationships, so no matter how much murder and mayhem is created by these women, her husband is there, both in character and out. I'm reminded of the traveling theater companies of the Spanish Golden Age, where women were allowed onstage, but only if their husbands or fathers were in the company too. There is, of course, the titillation of imagining we are watching these celebrity couples fight ("just like us") and also the stimulation of knowing that this Medea and Jason really do have sex. The marriages – onstage and off – develop richness and complexity. Still, as far as I can tell, no one has ever advertised casting real-life couples as the Capulets or the Lomans. When the wife murders or rages, the offstage husband suggests some control.

[12] I am grateful to Sarah McCarroll (email correspondence) for this observation.

As Ranald points out about Katherine and Petruchio, the Elizabethan performance might have been different with all boys, "since the original performance had men and boys beating each other in high-spirited combat there is nothing for feminists to worry about" (Ranald, 1994: 223). It is hard for me to imagine early modern performance as a golden age of no worrying for feminists, but it is certainly true that Shakespeare's plays are very different with women playing female characters. Female visibility seems to always invite a degree of control and containment. If it escaped notice when women played female parts, it became glaringly obvious when they were cast as male parts. Critics, a dominantly white male group as recent social media conversations have pointed out, writing about cross-gender casting in Shakespeare can be poetic and hysterical in their attempts to articulate their panic in a way that sounds intellectual. A taste will suffice:

- "So, while this hugely significant production has shown that numerous roles, major and minor, can henceforth ignore gender in their casting, it has not for me proved that there is no risk in swapping both genders in a romantic or sexual encounter" (Lister, 2016).
- "Theatre-land is play-land – we suspend disbelief, we let our imaginations run free. Increasingly, however, I worry that play-land is being patrolled by the Thought Police" (Cavendish, 2017b).
- "Casting a male actor as Princess Katherine to be wooed by a female Henry asks a lot of the audience I think, and the jury is still out on whether one can take gender blind casting that far" (Lister, 2016).
- "Contemplating this past week's big opening at The National – actress Tamsin Greig taking on the role of Malvolio in *Twelfth Night* – a strange, melancholy thought struck me. Is this curtains for the male actor?" (Cavendish, 2017a).

Curtains, indeed! The past five years have seen women seamlessly – not to say invisibly – taking on the roles of Kent, Mark Antony, and Henry V. These are not all-female productions of Shakespeare plays; the directors had to choose that this part would be played by a woman despite being traditionally a male character (against gender), just as they have to choose that this traditionally male part will be played by a man. If you set *Julius Caesar* in contemporary times, of course some of the senators should be female. The presence of female bodies can then be seen as a more realistic casting choice – the mirror held up to nature and the like. But which character is female makes a difference to the story that is being told. If Gloucester is a woman and Lear is a man, we are comparing parents; if Kent is a woman and Lear is a man, we are thinking about friendship and loyalty. I am not downplaying the joy of increased representation: it does something powerful to reclaim these roles for today, to bring these characters back to life and insist that today they could/should be women. I am arguing that the bodies still do not disappear (ask the critics cited previously) and that even when they are seamlessly integrated, they are powerfully visible.

The power of their bodies is partially evidenced by the anger that they arouse when they show up where they were not expected. In "Cross-Gender Casting as Feminist Interventions in the Staging of Early Modern Plays," Gemma Miller makes a very strong case that cross-gender casting, particularly in Shakespeare's history plays, "constitutes a bold feminist activism" (Miller, 2014: 4) because "it is only by de-gendering the traditionally male subject position through cross-gender casting that feminists can . . . demand to be taken seriously on the world stage, both literally and metaphorically" (Miller, 2014: 6). Gender is a funny thing to talk about in productions of Shakespeare because the plays were not written to be performed by females, so gender was written to be performed, as it wasn't "given" by the bodies of the actors. Women have often slipped quietly into the role of soldiers, nobles, or kids, and actors like Sarah Bernhardt or Helen Mirren have done celebrated star turns as Hamlet or Prospero. I want to focus on productions where cross-gender casting told stories not just about the character or gender itself but about theatrical production and hierarchy in general. Miller says that Lloyd's all-female *Julius Caesar* created "multiple layers of character and gender presented in one and the same body" and that this

> encouraged the spectator to focus on the process rather than the embodiment of representation. The result was neither a parodic impersonation of the opposite gender (as in Rylance's Olivia), nor a nineteenth-century "breeches" style of transvestism, designed to display, rather than veil,

the female form. By deconstructing the hierarchies of spectator and performer, subject and object, the actors were thus
able to disrupt male/female hierarchies and expose gender
as a discursive formation. (Miller, 2014: 12)

This is casting that invites us to imagine an alternate future, one without
a gender binary or inherited hierarchy, because we are made aware of the
process by which we create and reify these categories. Repeatedly seeing
and reimagining our categories allows us to build a different one. In
contemporary Shakespeare productions, we can see evidence of casting
that is not merely about shifting our perspective on the character but about
the story and the context of the production. When Michelle Terry cast
herself as Hamlet, for example, the "bold feminist activism" (Miller,
2014: 4) wasn't that she was Hamlet but that she did the casting.

In the summer of 2018, Michelle Terry became the artistic director of
Shakespeare's Globe and cast herself as Hamlet. The critics weren't uni-
versally kind. The *New York Times* claimed Terry's first season lacked "the
kind of guiding directorial hand that you expect these days, not least in
Shakespeare" (Wolf, 2018). The *Times of London* described Terry's interest
in "gender-neutral casting" as a "bee in her bonnet" (Hart, 2018). For those
for whom inclusive casting is about accurately representing the world
around us, Terry's first season – *Hamlet* and *As You Like It* in repertory –
was victorious. What is clear from reading the reviews, however, is that
there is no blindness to the gender, race, or physical abilities of the actors.
The common complaint about there not being a directorial hand speaks to,
I think, the ways in which the casting lacked a cohesive story being told by
these very visible bodies in these very well-known plays. The problem was
the attempt at representation rather than a strategic use of those bodies to
counter old biased, narrow-minded narratives about who could be whom.
In Terry's *Hamlet*, Ophelia was a slight young man, Horatio was a woman,
and her Guildenstern was deaf. Shubham Saraf's Ophelia was almost never
mentioned by critics, though Michael Billington found his Ophelia to have
a "dangerous anger" (Billington, 2018). This casting choice interested me
because having a male body play Ophelia made the character's oppression
more visible. He seemed more breakable than Hamlet from the start. I spent

some time trying to figure out why Guildenstern was deaf or why Rosencrantz was a much older man. It must be that I should just learn to see these things differently, but that just made me wonder about the other casting: Why isn't Polonius female? Why is Horatio white?

The casting that was most important at the Globe in 2018, it turns out, wasn't who was onstage; it was the casting of Michelle Terry as the new Artistic Director. As Valerie Clayman Pye has pointed out, coming in after Emma Rice's contentious run, Terry had to establish herself as both new and also a part of a long line of Shakespearean actors/directors.[13] Thus she had to play Hamlet. By casting herself as Hamlet, she was casting herself as the inheritor not of Rice but of Mark Rylance, Kenneth Branagh, Lawrence Olivier, Henry Irving, Richard Burbage. She may not be the first female to play Hamlet, but she's the first female Artistic Director to play Hamlet. Her role as Artistic Director of the Globe will now be ghosted by her performance of Hamlet, and that will last longer than her performance as Hamlet. The character I believe Terry was building when she played Hamlet was Intellectual Leader and Director for the Globe of tomorrow. As Peter J. Smith has noted, "Shakespeare, if justly deployed, constitutes one of the most empowering tools for undoing pernicious and destructive prejudice" (quoted in Miller, 2014: 9). The way to justly deploy Shakespeare is through strategic counter casting both on and off the stage.

To recast theatrical leadership and directorial voice, Teresa Rebeck also cast a female *Hamlet*. Rebeck's *Bernhardt/Hamlet* uses the historical fact of Sarah Bernhardt's playing Hamlet as an opportunity to look at the fictions of gender. Janet McTeer's tall Bernhardt, additionally elevated in black leather boots, takes center stage, demanding that Rostand rewrite *Hamlet* for her. She controls the narrative and unmasks Hamlet, revealing that he doesn't have a whole lot of masculine in him. This Bernhardt was actor, critic, dramaturg, director, and producer. As Jesse Green notes in the *Times*, "The gender crisis

---

[13] "Gender-Blind, Race-Blind, Ability-Blind Casting at Shakespeare's Globe," Shakespeare: Recent Innovations in Casting, Association for Theatre in Higher Education Conference, August 8, 2019. Unpublished conference paper. I am grateful for Valerie Clayman Pye's insights in this paper and her forthcoming work on Terry and the Globe.

even then, 'Bernhardt/Hamlet' suggests, was not about femaleness but maleness. What's wrong with men that they can't tolerate strong women? . . . In letting Bernhardt dissect *Hamlet* in rehearsal – to ask why, undressing him, she never finds a man – the play locates a marvelous side door to its subject" (Green 2018). This might be the side door to *Hamlet*, but it's the front door to Rebeck's play. Rebeck's play uses a famous example of counter casting not to argue that a woman can play Hamlet but that a woman can run a theater. She was bossy, creative, and controlling of the men around her. The play is not about her Hamlet but about her taking on a part not meant for her and demonstrating that she deserves to be there, even if she's hated for it. The success of the play and McTeer's performance can be found in the *New Criterion*'s vitriolic review of the production, which began by suggesting that if Rebeck wanted to do something like *Shakespeare in Love* (1998), she should have cast "dewy" Gwyneth Paltrow instead of "the fifty-seven-year-old Janet McTeer," who Kyle Smith describes as "an androgynous, brittle, frosty six-footer, she has an angular, avian quality. I'd cast her as a Nazi prison guard or maybe a street lamp" (2018). Had Paltrow played the part, the character would not have been the same; Paltrow's Bernhardt would have been demure and charming, allowed through the doors of power because she asked so nicely. McTeer's Bernhardt, on the other hand, suggested an unwelcome power and authority for Smith. McTeer was not his only problem with the play, though: "Not that the most luscious actress on earth could have saved this wretched play" (Smith 2018). Like Mitch McConnell complaining that he told Senator Elizabeth Warren to stop speaking but, "Nevertheless, she persisted," such criticism is a sign that the casting, if not the play, succeeded. Had McTeer's performance not staged such a vivid depiction of what it might/will look like to have women refuse the ingenue role and take center stage (onstage and off), perhaps Smith wouldn't have been so angry.

2.3 Differently Abled Bodies Onstage

One can hear a similar resistance to change in this review of *Macbeth* at the Globe in 2016: "The central roles were played as nature intended. But there was a fascinating piece of casting lower down the pecking order. The porter, who has his (usually) one solo scene of comedy, was played by a woman, Nadia Albina, who has a handicap: her right arm finishes at the elbow" (Lister, 2016). I'm not sure what "nature intended" or how a "pecking order" works in *Macbeth* or if Albina's casting is more radical for her vagina or for her "handicapped" arm. The hypervisibility of both, though, speaks to the presumption of whiteness, maleness, and a normative body. This visibility might affront some critics, but it does draw attention to this presumption, thus allowing directors to challenge the normality and invisibility of white, male bodies. Directors are casting increasingly more actors with disabilities or differently-abled bodies and, not unlike casting different races or genders in Shakespeare, sometimes this contributes to the sense of an accurate representation of the community and other times it tells a new story through differently casting an old play.

Disabled characters have not been rarities onstage or film, but disabled actors have been. The practice of actors pretending to have disability has generated critical backlash. Christine Bruno notes that this "cripping up" or "cripface" has historically been rewarded by the Academy Awards: "since the ceremony's inception in 1929, as of 2011, nineteen percent of Academy Award for Best Actor winners have received the coveted statue for playing a disabled character. . . . [J]ust two of those winners were, themselves, disabled actors" (Bruno, 2019: 86). This high percentage of winners doesn't surprise me, as spectators seem to love it when the privileged actor performs the vulnerability of the less privileged; the joke I remember hearing was that white women win Oscars by gaining weight and not wearing make-up and white men win by playing a disabled character. Bruno insists that it's long past time for disabled actors to take their rightful place onstage. As Wanda Strukus (2011) argued about the performance of Artie, a disabled teen in *Glee*, casting a nondisabled actor both missed an opportunity and also sacrificed artistic merit. To many in the disabled community, the actor's performance felt wrong; for example, he did not seem to dance in his chair like someone for whom the chair is an extension of self. When actors can pretend to be disabled like they pretend to be southern or a cowboy or on the run from the law, it suggests that disability is like a costume or an accent – something to put on or take off at will.

The problem with casting actors who are "faking" this alternate body is that it limits what we can imagine or know about differently abled bodies. The casting of an able-bodied actor in the role of Artie, for example, allowed spectators to continue to believe that they knew what the experience is, that it was accessible to them with an imagination and a chair. As Ali Stroker showed as Ado Annie, an actor for whom dancing, pursuing, flirting, and thinking always includes the chair will invite us to see the limits of the character, of the human, differently.[14] It's no longer a metaphor of a "handicap"; it's truly a differently abled body. As Carrie Sandahl recognizes, "It is difficult to turn disability into a metaphor when it is literally embodied" (Sandahl, 2019: 89). This, then, requires us to think about all bodies differently. In productions of Shakespeare, casting differently abled actors in roles that have not been traditionally marked as "disabled" or different can expand the community of people included in the telling of critical stories right now. Sometimes, though, when the particularity of the actor's body shoots the play through with new meaning or resonance, it can also crack open an old play in a new way.

The production of *The Two Noble Kinsmen* at the Globe in 2018 did not make me like the play, but it did provide me with an opportunity to dislike myself and challenge my assumptions. Director Barrie Rutter cast Francesca Mills, an extraordinarily talented actor/dancer/singer who is 3'8", as the Jailer's Daughter. The story is basically about how desire for one woman destroys a wonderful friendship between two princes and the desire of another woman for one of these princes makes her go mad. The lesson seems to be that male friendship is far more valuable and noble than what is available with women. As Andrezej Lukowski put it in his review for *Time Out*, "In its blithe misogyny, 'The Two Noble Kinsmen' verges on being as problematic as the more popular 'The Taming of the Shrew' or 'The Merchant of Venice', only without the redeeming feature of being a good play" (Lukowski, 2018). The Jailer's Daughter is the powerless and frustrated "wench" who loves and desires Palamon, the prince who does not return her feelings. According to one critic, Mills "brings an extravagant physicality to the jailer's daughter, amplifying both the comedy of her

---

[14] See also Patrick McKelvey's history of acting training at the National Theatre Workshop of the Handicapped, started in 1977, and the connection made between "disability and authenticity in the US political and cultural imagination" (McKelvey, 2019; 83).

unbridled lust, and her desperate disorientation as she loses her mind" (Everett, 2018); another calls the performance "a star-making turn" (Shenton, 2018); and a third says she uses "physicality in her scenes to play the comedy as well as the tragedy of a women who doesn't get to choose in life. Her sadness and lunacy is a connecting thread through the scenes and she is a remarkable stage presence; funny, engaging, relatable while delivering well-balanced pathos" (Bowie-Sell, 2018). She is and she did indeed steal the show, but her stature was not invisible to the spectators.

When she is rejected by Palamon, there is a different pity. When she talks about the frustration and powerlessness of being a teenage girl in one of her four soliloquies, the audience hears it differently. As she says of her desire for Palamon, "to marry him is hopeless, / To be his whore is witless. Out upon't, / What pushes are we wenches driven to / When fifteen once has found us!" (2.3.4–8). After she joins the morris dancers for an extraordinary performance before the court, all the dancers leave the stage and she is left onstage. She turns to follow them out, and the doors are shut on her. In the performance I saw, there was an audible "aaaah" from the audience that seemed to catch us all off guard. I wondered if I was hearing the same sound that would be made if a puppy or small child had been spurned. This, not the dance, was how the director chose to end the act: the audience audibly pitying this woman despite the strength and power she had just displayed in the dance. I rewatched the production a year later, and the taped audience had the same reaction: pity followed by silence and discomfort. I am out on a limb here presuming this reaction was shared, so let me speak for myself: catching myself demeaning her with my pity called my attention to my own ableism and invited me to rethink that reaction, those assumptions. Further, it shifted my perspective on the play because I began to see what Shakespeare and Fletcher depict as the moral and intellectual weakness of women as the misogyny it is. Or perhaps, as theater scholar Sarah McCarroll suggested, her performance up until that moment did not allow us to pity her; she had clearly and confidently made her way through the world, making it work for her, "until she failed in love." When the door slammed in her face, the character that I had built for her was suddenly unable to continue, and I was surprised to find the condescending compassion within myself that her performance heretofore had kept at bay. Her hypervisible body and our hyperaudible response to it demonstrated that it is not love, or the female sex, or desire, or rejection that is the problem; it is our narrow-minded reactions that need to change. Mills can never "disappear into a role," as many have claimed is the mark of acting superiority; her visibility creates a powerful reclaiming of an old role for a new kind of future where, for me at least, ableist and sexist assumptions are made visible and our categories of who gets to love, be loved, and steal the show are expanded.

Also at the Globe in 2018, Nadia Nadarajah played Celia in *As You Like It* and Guilderstern in *Hamlet*. Both characters are part of communicative couples – Celia and Rosalind, of course, "have slept together, / Rose at an instant, learn'd, play'd, eat together, / And wheresoever we went, like Juno's swans, / Still [they] went coupled and inseparable" (1.3.73–76), and Rosencrantz and Guildenstern are practically thought of as one character in two bodies. Critics loved Nadarajah as Celia: "Celia, Rosalind's devoted sidekick, is played by the enormously expressive deaf actress Nadia Nadarajah, who signs her lines – only some of which are translated. (So lucid is she as a performer that the character's intentions are entirely clear throughout)" (Wolf, 2018). Her performance as Guildenstern, understandably, got less comment. While I loved watching her onstage and thought that the idea of R&G sharing communication was as rich in potential as Celia and Rosalind, I did not like her casting as Guildenstern. Primarily this was because the need to translate Guildenstern's lines for the King and Queen slowed down the rhythm of the poetry without adding to the scene. When we have to wait to hear "Faith, her privates we" (2.2.234), the timing of the joke is sacrificed only to have us wonder why Rosencrantz and Hamlet need that translated. They don't. The translation is for the spectators, but with the joke ruined, we are left trying to find thematic meaning in the line. When Celia's translations require waiting, our attention is brought to her and to her efforts to keep up with Rosalind, constrain Rosalind, and comment on Rosalind. Her "voice" becomes crucial, worth waiting for, and also, for those who don't understand sign language, split between her body and the translator. This generates ideas and possible interpretations for me with Celia but does not work as well with Guildenstern.

If Rosencrantz and Guildenstern were both deaf and their lines were never translated for the audience – perhaps Denmark all spoke sign language – and so they were this dual space of silence and mystery, that would bring my attention to the place of "words" in this world and the silent spying. Rosencrantz, played by Pearce Quigley, is much older than Nadarajah, and I found myself wondering how the two of them became friends – let alone how they are meant to be "so neighbor to [Hamlet's] youth and havior" (2.212) – so the *pair* felt miscast, more than the specificity of Nadarajah's body. In 2016, Nadarajah wrote an essay for a website on the use of signing onstage, arguing that sign language onstage should be "clear, fluent and in keeping with the style of the production so that it becomes a part of the artistic vision of the production and not just an afterthought for access, or thrown in because it looks pretty" (Nadarajah, 2016). She referred to this essay in an interview with Terry during rehearsals for *As You Like It* and *Hamlet*, insisting on the "dramaturgical and aesthetic underpinning for the use of sign language" (Nadarajah, 2016). The two plays cast the same talented actor, the same use of language, but the dramaturgical and aesthetic implications were very different.

The same can be said for the deaf and hearing-impaired actors in Sam Gold's production of *King Lear* with Glenda Jackson. The Duke of Cornwall is played by Russell Harvard, a deaf actor who is accompanied by an Aide who translates for him. It is this Aide who tries to stop him from taking Gloucester's second eye, and their confrontation about it takes place all in sign language – the stage silent except for occasional groans of pain from Gloucester. Cornwall's part and voice are divided: the body stands in one place and his lines come from someone over there. This is highlighted when Goneril forces Gloucester's face to turn to Cornwall, not the translator. She holds the character together as one, though other hearing characters conflate the voice/lines of the character with the person speaking them out loud. As fascinating as I found this, I couldn't connect it to anything else in the staging of the play. The need for translation hinders the pace and prosody; all during act one, if Cornwall was onstage, the other actor was translating what was being said, even if it wasn't being said to him. Because I found my attention pulled away from where the dialogue was to watch the quickly moving hands upstage, I spent the scene thinking about it from Cornwall's perspective, since the director clearly wanted us to see him take in the information. But that didn't reward exegesis – the play doesn't belong to Cornwall – and so I started thinking about the actor, who might need the lines translated the first time but surely knows the play by now. Can't the translator take a rest until it's his cue? Having a deaf actor do the blinding in silence made a painful moment differently resonant, but having the signing upstage the fall of the kingdom suggested a different narrative or thematic intent.

Directors like Terry are creating Shakespearean worlds onstage that are as diverse and interesting as the streets around us in London and New York. Perhaps I shouldn't ask "why" Cornwall is now deaf just as I don't ask why he wasn't before. Certainly, the conventions have changed with casting so that spectators expect a larger diversity in the casting and reviewers rarely mention the lack of realism in casting. In his review of Ruth Negga as Hamlet in the Gate Theatre of Dublin's production at St. Ann's Warehouse in 2020, Ben Brantley noted the way her body/sex mattered differently:

> Hamlet is portrayed by the Ethiopian-Irish actress Ruth Negga, and the double-sidedness of this most complex of Shakespeare's heroes has rarely been better served. I started to write that the fact that this man is played by a woman is irrelevant. But there is one sense in which the basic disparity between this actress and this role feeds the quickening sensibility that infuses every aspect of Farber's interpretation, which cannily condenses and rearranges the text for speed and focus. For what is conveyed here with glittering incisiveness is the work's sense of life as theater, in which playing roles expands and constricts the possibilities in being human. In this world, Negga's Hamlet rules as the Player Prince. (Brantley, 2020)

When Negga enters, mourning King Hamlet, it is not clear whether she will be playing a male or female version of Hamlet. She is small and thin and could easily be a young man. Then the entire cast comes on, all wearing the same costume – black pants, white shirt, black jacket – and standing together facing the audience, as if to invite us to see them all as actors, rather than differentiated by gender. We see and don't see the actors' bodies; they both are and are not the characters. What is central is not the relationships or the bodies or the social-historical context, but rather the extraordinary grief in a rotten Denmark.

Casting is like categorizing: we group things together so as to simplify our cognitive load. I don't need to understand how to operate each and every door I run into; it fits the category of "door," so I behave as if they are all the same. This may not work for all doors all the time, but it gives me a good guess. In the 1970s, Eleanor Rosch (1998), a psychologist at the University of California, Berkeley, showed that categories are defined by prototypes, not a list of rules or qualifications. This means that our category of "doctor" may be defined by white coat on a white man, but it can be expanded to include the young Indian woman who enters holding our lab results. Based on years of studying color recognition in speakers of the Dani tribe in New Guinea, Rosch and colleagues showed that although the Dani speakers did not have words for certain colors, they could see them and have a conceptual category for them; their language did not wholly determine their conceptual system. Thus, she argues, "human categorization should not be considered the arbitrary product of historical accident or of whimsy but rather the result of psychological principles of categorization, which are subject to investigation" (Rosch, 1998: 251). What the investigations concluded is that our thinking is constrained by our categorization – and our language – but not defined by it. In other words, we may see all the colors, but we attend to the colors we have names for. Categories do not expand easily, however, as people assume that they are based on an objectively-assessed set of shared properties, in which case changing what or whom belongs in the category of "door" or "president" cannot happen easily.

That is the political power of casting: it helps us challenge and expand our categories. Judi Dench became Bond's M in 1995, and spectators recognized her authority, intelligence, and experience as close enough to the prototypical M that her gender was uncontroversial. When Dennis Haysbert was cast as presidential-candidate David Palmer, spectators understood that *24* took place in the near future – one where the category of president was not limited to the white prototype. What casting directors saw in Judi Dench or Dennis Haysbert was what the American people are looking for in their political candidates: someone who can "hold" and maintain authority. This is a category that is not fixed; it can, and must, be changed. Studio heads have traditionally thought that a successful film required a white male to "carry the film." However, this is starting to change: according to a study by the Annenberg Inclusion Initiative, of the 100 top films in 2018, thirty-nine had a female lead or co-lead, up from 33 in 2017. And the top-grossing film of 2018 was *Black Panther*. Ideas about who can "hold" power and who can "carry the film" remain constrained by gender, race, and ability. A strategic attention to performances – in fiction or in life – that don't seem "right," that stretch, extend, or break what seems like the "right casting," allows us to see casting as a way to blur or transform categories.

3 The Years of Five Lears

> When a man has power, we take it for granted. But when a woman has power, we're forced to look at the nature of power itself.
>
>   Ruth Maleczech (who played a female Lear in 1987)[15]

James Shapiro's *The Year of Lear* lays out the context of Shakespeare's writing of the play, a time of "many ills besetting mainstream English culture in the early seventeenth century: a world of callous and self-righteous male authorities, of casual violence and willful deception . . . a disturbing social world not all that far from the one imagined in *King Lear*" (Shapiro, 2015: 81). Although the information we have about Shakespeare is minimal, Shakespeare's world in 1606 is well-documented. Shapiro sees the impact of the new monarch, a Scottish King bent on uniting Great Britain, in the play's divided kingdom: "From its opening scene, when a map of Britain is brought onstage, King Lear wrestles with what Britishness means, especially in relationship to the long-standing national identities it superseded" (Shapiro, 2015: 43). Though thwarted, "the Gunpowder Plot was producing nightmares, tapping deep into Jacobean political and religious anxieties" (Shapiro, 2015: 127). The "play's cruel logic," Shapiro argues, fits its times. For Shapiro, *King Lear* is an inevitable product of its moment: King James's interest in witchcraft, the terror experienced with the discovery of the Gunpowder Plot, and the

---

[15]   Quoted in Cavendish, 2017a.

devastation of the Plague in 1606. Directors choose plays to direct that they believe speak to the present moment; when many directors turn to the same play, it is worth considering how the play might help spectators respond to this particular moment of heightened chaos.

During the years between 2017 and 2019, I saw five productions of *King Lear*. In interviews included in the National Theatre Live's broadcast of the Ian McKellan *King Lear* from 2018, actors reflected the resonances with Brexit and Trump, as if echoing Shapiro's description of Lear's end: "For Lear – and for playgoers – at play's end, authority is shown to be arbitrary, its 'great image' a beggar running from a barking dog" (Shapiro, 2015: 87). The guiding argument of much of my previous work on Shakespeare is that plays in performance operate as a kind of cognitive prosthetic, through which the community comes to see, and thus to know, new ways of thinking about challenging problems. I'm not alone in making this argument; Mary Crane's recent *Losing Touch with Nature* (2014) shows how Shakespeare's plays facilitate a painful shift from Aristotelian thinking about nature and the cosmos to the radical atomism of Thomas Harriot and others and the heliocentrism of Copernicus and Galileo. *King Lear*, in particular, seems to grapple with critical questions around atomism and nothingness, the scientific method, age and the patriarchy. Through the performance of *King Lear*, spectators could see and experience challenging epistemological problems of their day. Ellen Spolsky (2015b) and Alva Noë (2015) make this argument about art in general: that it is a tool to think with. If theater provides us a tool to think with, what might these five productions of *King Lear* be asking us to think differently about? Before I discuss the productions, I will talk about how I see *King Lear* as a prime example of how theater demonstrates embodied cognition.

To review, King Lear wants to retire so as, he thinks, to crawl unburdened toward death. He splits his kingdom in three (never a good idea) and asks his daughters to descant on how much they love him in order to get their share of the kingdom. Cordelia, when asked, says "nothing" in response to Lear's question, "What can you say to draw a third more opulent than your sisters? Speak" (1.1.85–86). This "nothing" costs Cordelia her dowry, as well as her land. In the end, pretty much everyone is dead and Lear enters carrying his dead daughter, Cordelia, determined to prove that she is not dead. It is in these two incredibly theatrical moments – Cordelia telling her father "nothing" and Lear trying to find evidence of life in his dead daughter – where the play stages an idea of time and matter, wait and weight, enabling his audience to see it "feelingly" (4.6.145).

The exchange between Lear and his daughter at the start of the play about "nothing" rewards scanning:

> LEAR: What can you say to draw
>   A third more opulent than your sisters?
>   Speak.
> CORDELIA: Nothing, my lord.
> LEAR: Nothing?
> CORDELIA: Nothing.
> LEAR: Nothing can come of nothing.
>   Speak again.
>
> (1.1.85–90)

The middle three lines, which should go together to form one pentameter line, are two syllables short. This means that there is a pause in there somewhere – but where that absence is implicates the meaning. What's not said, what's not there, changes the meaning depending on where that wait is. Cordelia could take a pause before her first or second "nothing," or Lear could take a pause before his first or second "nothing." During dialogue like this, if an actor pauses, it makes the audience attend to the perspective of the character: What is the character thinking that causes a delay in the turn taking, back and forth? If Cordelia pauses before her first line, we imagine that she has not yet decided how to respond. If she responds right away but then pauses before the second "nothing," we think that the first "nothing" was impulsive and the second is a decision – one word and two different meanings. If the pause belongs to Lear, our attention is drawn to the impact this is having on the king, rather than on the reasoning and experience of Cordelia leading to her response. Either way, the pause – a lack of words and sound – influences the meaning we are making about this "nothing." In this way, Shakespeare is able to stage, at the beginning of the play, what Lear only realizes at its end: something most assuredly comes from nothing.

When Lear enters in act five carrying Cordelia, he spends the majority of his dying breath trying to conceive of the death of his daughter. He first declares that she is dead but then doubts his own perception; he asks for a mirror to make sure: "I know when one is dead, and when one lives. / She's dead as earth. Lend me a looking glass. / If that her breath will mist or stain the stone, / Why, then she lives" (5.3.261–264). When the mirror fails to bring the sign of life for which he is so desperate, Lear repeats his experiment with a feather hoping for different results: "This feather stirs, she lives! If it be so, / It is a chance which does redeem all sorrows / That ever I have felt" (5.3.266–67). What he "knows" has broken down and so he must perform an experiment. If x happens, then y will be true. Moreover, these are experiments staged for the members of the court still living: they are his spectators. They can validate his experiment through witnessing it. Though his words fail him, he turns to scientific observation and the performance of the experiment to understand what his mind cannot conceive. But why does this work? Why assume that the events are linked? A feather stirring is not the same as a daughter's life. But connected through breath, the two spaces are related. Without mapping the movement of the feather to what it represents, no sorrows will be redeemed. How do we know what we think we know?[16]

We feel it: when one actor carries another actor onstage, we know what is nothing and what is something. This moving Pietà, the father cradling a grown woman the way he may have cradled the baby she once was, breaks our heart because we know it, we do not just perceive it. *King Lear* offers its viewers a way to rethink an issue, as Crane shows, of critical concern to Elizabethans of the time. As Spolsky argues, "Quite independent of authorial intentions, a culture's most valued works of imagination can just occasionally be caught in the act of responding to structural failure by re-representing difficult issues in locally significant forms – forms that themselves evolve to adumbrate new possibilities" (Spolsky, 2015a: 34). The theatricalization of the story stages the cognitive leap it is asking us to make. What we see, hear, and imagine still must be staged and embodied in order to be known.

[16] I discuss some elements of this in "If: Lear's Feather and the Staging of Science" (Cook, 2011).

I have rarely seen a production of this play where there is only one pause taken in that exchange of nothings in act one. Contemporary actors and theater directors do not follow the implicit instructions of the poetry, and the magnitude of this moment seems to invite both actors to take pauses, making the presence of this nothing less palpable than it is as written. Contemporary audiences listen to the poetry, to the pauses, but also look to the actors playing Lear and Cordelia to understand what may be behind this "nothing." This is particularly true if the director cuts Cordelia's asides during her sisters' speeches of love – as Jonathan Munby did in McKellen's production for the National Theatre Live. If she hasn't invited the audience into her perspective through these asides, her rejection of her father is the first we hear from her and she is distinguished from her older sisters only by her father's clear preference for her ("our joy, / Although the last, not least"; 1.1.82–83) and by her response to his request. In two of the productions – Ian McKellen's and Anthony Sher's – Cordelia is played by a black actor, possibly to suggest that her mother was different from Reagan's and Goneril's, which might explain her being special in her father's eyes. McKellen mentioned in an interview that, although it wasn't meant to be visible to the audience, he wore two wedding rings, signifying his second marriage to Cordelia's mother.[17] Whether spectators look to her parentage to explain her difference, Cordelia's "nothing" invites them to see her as different. For spectators with any degree of familiarity with the play, Cordelia's physical "something" is also central: we wonder whether or not this Lear will be able to carry this Cordelia after more than two exhausting hours onstage. While Shakespeare encodes the relationship in the poetry, contemporary directors tell the story in casting.

The bodies chosen to tell the story today are critical to understanding the epistemological question at the heart of *Lear*. Casting Lear defines any production of *Lear*, though recent productions seem interested in using the casting not to focus on the man or the mental state of the man, but rather the social system that defines and contains the men and women within it. Sir Donald Wolfit's famous advice to any actor who had been cast as Lear was

---

[17] See www.youtube.com/watch?v=ahFtoCq6CHw.

to "[g]et a light Cordelia and keep an eye on the Fool" (RSC, 2020).[18] In an article for *The Guardian* in 2014, Jonathan Pryce wrote, "Tradition dictates that you should play Lear while you're young enough to lift Cordelia up and carry her" (Barnett, 2014). None of the *King Lear*s I've seen in the last three years have taken this advice – one dragged Cordelia and another pushed her on a wagon. Ian McKellan's 2018 *King Lear* for the National Theatre reprised his role from a few years earlier and was broadcast throughout 2019. Anthony Hopkins's *King Lear* was released on Amazon in May of 2018. Anthony Sher's production with the Royal Shakespeare Company was brought to New York's Brooklyn Academy of Music in 2018. In Toronto, the Groundling Theatre produced *Lear* in 2018 with Seana McKenna in the title role. Glenda Jackson brought her *King Lear* from London to New York in 2019. What are these five *Lear*s saying to us now? What can we learn about this play and our current time by looking at how five productions in roughly the same moment cast this play? These *Lear*s represent a vacated patriarchy that in the end is not even paternal.

Charles Lamb famously argued that the play was "unactable" because the drama wasn't about a physical man but about the mind: "The greatness of Lear is not in corporal dimension, but in intellectual . . . on the stage we see nothing but corporal infirmities and weakness, the impotence of rage; while we read it, we see not Lear, but we are Lear, we are in his mind" (Lamb, 1811, cited in Taylor and Egan, 2016: 2349). Contemporary productions are less interested in being in Lear's mind. In his review of *Performing King Lear: Gielgud to Russell Beale* by Jonathan Croall, Paul Menzer notes, "But failure – the failure to stage a storm, the failure to look the 'right' age, the failure to carry Cordelia – is the hallmark of the play's performance history, a sort of masochistic celebration of heroic but doomed assaults on the play" (Menzer, 2017: 208). Like Hamlet, Lear is considered a necessary achievement for an actor of a certain age and caliber. So perhaps it was inevitable that Sher, McKellen, and Hopkins would take on Lear at roughly the same time. All three men were very good as Lear, but none of them illuminated the character for me – perhaps because in the age of Trump and Brexit, I have less patience for and interest in old men causing

---

[18] This is how he is quoted on the RSC's website; I've also heard other variations.

massive trouble for their kingdoms and then being sad that they were also impacted by their poor choices. I realize this is an unfair depiction of Lear, but that is simply not the part of the story I am interested in. I am not alone in this; Elisabeth Vincentelli, in her review of Sher's Lear at Brooklyn Academy of Music for the *New York Times*, also thought of Trump:

> And that I started rooting for Goneril and, to a lesser extent, Regan is indicative, perhaps, of the unconscious influence of our current national mood. After all, the sisters may have endured Lear's arbitrary whims for years, and they have seen him reject his youngest daughter, Cordelia (Mimi Ndiweni), after she refused to praise him. (Vincentelli, 2018)

No matter who played Lear, I found myself focusing on the leadership of women in the play. Emma Thompson as Goneril against Anthony Hopkins's Lear made this sister a leading lady – certainly she has played across from Hopkins in *Howard's End* (1992) and *Remains of the Day* (1993), so this association will haunt, in Carlson's terms (2001), this casting anyway. Claire Price, Goneril to McKellen's Lear, seemed like the clear head of state; her sister, Kristy Bushell's Regan, on the other hand, compensated for a lack of political polish with the force of a cocky athlete or movie producer. Her gender was clear but evinced the sexual confidence of man used to abusing his power. McKellen's Kent was played by Sinead Cusack, who then disguises as a man – though "not entirely convincingly," as the *Variety* Review claims (Trueman, 2017). All three of the productions with male Lears depict Cordelia in military gear at the end, suggesting that the military threat to Cornwall and Albany is not her husband France but her. This Cordelia was meant to lead men; in all of the productions, I felt like her refusal to say more than "nothing" at the love trial was not petulance but integrity. When the Lears say, in these productions, "I gave you all," I found myself nodding in agreement with the Regans, who interrupt to retort "and in good time you gave it" (2.4.250).

The Groundling Theatre's *Lear* with Seana McKenna told a new story with an old play. A well-known Canadian actor, McKenna had played a "splendidly oily, androgynous Richard III" at the Stratford Shakespeare

Festival in 2011, but this time, as one reviewer noted, "there's no gender impersonation involved, only gender swapping. Lear has become a queen, a matriarch and – in director Graham Abbey's semi-contemporary staging – a power-suited executive figure with a passing resemblance to Hillary Clinton or Theresa May" (Morrow, 2018). While I disagree about the evocation of Clinton or May, there is no question that the casting in this production powerfully spoke to the future. A female Lear is not just nontraditional casting or a concept gimmick for a production; it's using casting to go back to move forward. The casting in this *Lear* illuminated how some of our categories are different now and how others maybe should be.

McKenna holds authority well, so when she enters at the start to divide her kingdom, she does not seem wrong to be in charge. This Lear seems more wrong as a parent than as a leader. When she asks her daughters to perform the ridiculous love declaration, we are sad for all of them to have grown up with this cold narcissist. Despite the reviewer finding Clinton or May in the performance, I found no attempt evoke the two leaders – other than that it was a white woman of a certain age. Yet this may be enough, as we rarely get to see women of a certain age in positions of power that are not contested. This Lear is not a contemporary female politician, who would have to smile and avoid being called a bitch; this is a female queen who is not afraid of her power or her leadership. As with her male counter-part, this Lear is undone by her daughters. When King Lear said, "I gave you all" (3.1.249), for example, it referred to the kingdom, the titles, the money; when mom said it, it referred to *all*. As Susan G. Cole said in her review, "When an outraged Lear declares to her daughters, 'I gave you all,' she's now talking about not only her property but her physical body. And so, when she curses them, wishing them barrenness, she knows exactly what she hopes they never experience" (Cole, 2018). This Lear seems wounded and destroyed by the way her daughters insist that she is old and the ways in which life discards women of this age. This woman, this Lear, reunites with Gloucester by rubbing up on his leg in a masturbation gesture that asserts her sexuality and authority in a similar – and similarly troubling – way as some men. Seeing this old woman in the spotlight is different; it's radical. Our categories of leader, human, older woman, must be expanded in this light.

These productions use the bodies of the actors cast to examine the epistemological chasm of the shifting notions of gender. Although I felt this in the productions with the male Lears, it was the McKenna *Lear* that shifted the story for me to focusing on the femininity of power. Glenda Jackson's *King Lear* in March 2019, however, staged the possibility of an end to gender. She walks onstage, this small woman in her eighties in a suit and short hair, and if it weren't for the fact that we were all here to see her Lear, it would not be clear if this Lear was a male or female. What is clear is that she is old: I say this not as an insult but rather because women on stage and screen rarely look this old, even if they occasionally get to be this age and still perform. Her performance was virtuosic, if not particularly nuanced; her ungendered power came both with and despite her age. Jackson's return to Broadway to play this apex of male Shakespearean characters occasioned a lot of press notice; in each interview or article I read, she is quoted as saying some version of the following: "Now, I wasn't interested in the gender-bender aspect, but what I did find interesting is how age begins to fracture those absolutes which tell you what women are and what men are" (Kachka, 2018). Jackson is talking about the story her body tells without her psychology; it is not her individual experience as a mother or father or a politician she is bringing to this performance – nor any actual feeling or response to any of those things. Jackson's portrayal is of genderless authority, and this comes from the way her body can tell the story. Seeing this staged and possible – this seemingly genderless leader – invites me to imagine an epistemological chasm where the jealously guarded idea of self and gender dissolve and what remains is the "unaccommodated" human.[19]

In Jackson's *Lear*, we have moved from a focus on the psychology of the individual to the social ecosystem that controls age and gender. Gloucester, Kent, and Edmund start the play, first with the court gossip about which of Cordelia's suitors the king prefers and then with a conversation about Gloucester's enjoyable adulterous romp with Edmund's mother that produced Gloucester's begrudgingly acknowledged bastard. Gloucester, here,

---

[19] This is very similar to the experience of Ruth Negga's *Hamlet*: when the specific psychology and gender of the character is no longer attended to, we are left with the generalizable and inevitable grief, end, despair.

is played by Jayne Houdyshell in short hair and a suit. She is playing Gloucester as a man, but the audience can tell from her body and her name in the program that she is a woman. As director Sam Gold said, having Houdyshell play Gloucester, "allows you to see the patriarchal aspects of the play in some relief, to see it with women playing it" (McHenry, 2019). Gold echoes Maleczech here: arguing that casting a woman as the father bragging about the fun he had in conceiving his bastard son and blind to his "good" son's love estranges what we normalize when men do it. The body doesn't match the gender performance or the text of the play, destabilizing our idea of gender.

Theatrical characters – at least since the rise of realism–have tended to be strongly-delineated individuals. In other words, the dramaturgy attends to the singular man or woman and his or her challenges, psychology, triumph, or fall. When Linda insists at Willy Loman's funeral that "attention must be paid," Arthur Miller, through Linda, is arguing that despite the challenges of the family and changes in economic/social structure of society, the work and value of the *individual* man must be respected. Characters have been important in theater because they were singular.[20] In Stanley Cavell's "The Avoidance of Love," he moves from a reading of *King Lear* to a discussion of the phenomenon of theatrical performance and the challenge it poses to reason and knowledge itself: "How do we learn that what we need is not more knowledge but the willingness to forgo knowing?" (Cavell, 2008: 324). The impossibility of the singularity of character – the essential whole of the self – can be evident as we watch Sarah Siddons, as Desdemona, die night after night: "You can say that there are two women, Mrs. Siddons and Desdemona, both of whom are mortal, but only one of whom is dying in front of our eyes. But what you have produced is two names. Not all the pointing in the world to *that* woman will distinguish the one woman from the other" (Cavell, 2008: 328). The psychological realism of Arthur Miller or Tennessee Williams, a dramaturgy of the internal causes

---

[20] For more on the idea of character in contemporary theater, see Elinor Fuchs, *The Death of Character: Perspectives on Theater after Modernism* (2000), and Christina Delgado-García, *Rethinking Character in Contemporary British Theatre* (2015).

that motivate the individual, is giving way to a theater that shifts our perspective from the "insides" of characters (wherein one finds their history or backstory) to the networks that connect us, that make us enact the event together. Directors of Shakespeare's plays may not change the words, but through changing the bodies being the characters, they are shifting our perspective. Jackson's body, her age, gender, and long history as a member of British Parliament, invites us to see leader and parent without gender. Through the casting of the female characters in the male Lears – and the male Lears' inability to carry any of the Cordelias – these directors drew my attention to the (potential) death of the patriarchy, less than the death of the patriarch.

4 Vision 2020

Human beings have told stories for longer than we have been writing, doing math, or creating art. Before we harnessed the horse or created an aqueduct, we pretended to be something we were not in order to tell about an alternate place and time. We came together as spectators, auditors, and jointly attended the storyteller, who we knew was one of us but for tonight was someone else. This play acting has taken different forms during different times; in addition to very different ideas of what qualified as good acting, the conventions for assigning roles in Shakespeare's time were very different than during the late nineteenth century, along with being very different from how casting is decided now. In this section, I turn to productions that invite us to reimagine what the self is – where it begins and ends – through casting in productions of Shakespeare. These productions, not unlike all the productions discussed in this book, are works of art in themselves: I am attending not to Shakespeare's play, but to how this director, this company, is telling that story now. Theater artists are providing us with opportunities to develop interpretive protocols that think about the story, the ecosystem, rather than the individual.

In the preceding sections, I have looked at some of the ways that directors are thinking with and through questions of gender, race, ability, and age to imagine a twenty-first-century self. The central argument is that directors are using casting as the central mode of meaning making in productions of Shakespeare. Whereas directors such as Adolphe Appia and Edward Gordon Craig and Peter Brook used the design of their productions of *Macbeth* or *Hamlet* or *A Midsummer Night's Dream* to tell the stories anew, contemporary directors use the bodies of the actors. I want to write about two Shakespeare productions that stage an evolution in our conceptual system, shifting our thinking from individuals telling stories to stories generating individuals. These productions invite us to reimagine what it can mean to feel and think as a group, rather than as an individual. It privileges the environment of the work's presentation rather than the backstory of its characters.

4.1 Unstable Selves

How we are invited to view the story has a significant impact on the story we see. Casting the spectator as participant alters the relationship between performer and spectator. In Pan Pan's production of *The Rehearsal: Playing the Dane*, the spectators are cast at a critical moment in a different role than "reader" of metaphoric experience; we are asked to physically stabilize the play's text by casting the title character – literally selecting which of the actors will be Hamlet tonight. Like many contemporary productions, the actors are onstage when we are led to our seats. They warm up, they read, they practice. A great dane – a dog, not the eponymous prince of Denmark – catches our attention, even if the actors don't. He is large and gorgeous – a small pony more than a dog. As anyone who knows anything about theater anticipates, this dog will upstage just about anything else that happens onstage with him. A woman starts the play by walking forward with pages and the leash of the dog. She introduces herself as a local Shakespearean scholar and reads an essay on the instability of the text of the play and the instability of the character of Hamlet. She mentions the much-discussed textual instability between the three versions of *Hamlet*, the "bad" Quarto, the "good" Quarto, and the Folio. The tortuous textual history of *Hamlet* means that editors can compare the Folios to the Quartos to investigate mysteries that previous editors or directors had erased through choice or correction. For example, in the First Quarto, the grave-digger's song refers to "such a ghest most meet" (Q1.16.34), though the Q2 and Folio emend it to "guest." Kathleen Irace points out that "ghest" might be a deliberate combination of "ghost" and "guest," as, in an earlier scene, Horatio asks Hamlet to "ceasen" his admiration for a while in order to take in Horatio's ghost report (Q1.2.106). "Season" – the choice of Q2 and the Folio text – makes as much sense as "cease in," so perhaps the Q1's combination allows both meanings to come into play. The scholar in Pan Pan's production refers to Hamlet's concern about his "too too sullied flesh": in the Folio, Hamlet's flesh is "solid"; in the First Quarto, it is "sallied"; and in the Second Quarto, his flesh is "sullied." Pan Pan's scholar wants to remind us of this indeterminacy as a key element to the play – a feature, not a bug. As expected, our attention returns again and again to the dog at her side – and she periodically must pet him, calm him – but this works to support her argument rather than to diminish our attention. We get the joke – the Great Dane that is both prince and dog, a reference to the destabilization that happens in serious scholarly ways and accidents of time.

She leaves with the dog, and the actors line up and a director assigns parts to the men and women standing downstage. Without any evidence, he tells the spectators that they are missing an actor. He comes down into the house and casts a spectator to play a part. He hands him a script and asks him to read this part when they get to it. They read the scene – actors in street clothes and the audience member barely distinguishable from them, except for the slightly more evident nerves he displays – and stop it almost as soon as the spectator's lines are completed. He is thanked and returned to his place among us, the audience. The director goes behind a table and commences an audition. Who will play Hamlet? Three different actors audition for the role of Hamlet, by reading a soliloquy or, in the case of one actor, reading a monologue from Samuel Beckett's *Endgame*. Once the auditions are done, the director confers with his associates and then tells the audience that they cannot decide who to cast so we must decide for them who will play Hamlet in tonight's production by coming onstage and standing behind the actor who we believe did the best job. We must bring our bodies into the drama. Once we are all up there, squeezing onstage, laughing at our discomfort and smiling sheepishly at the actor we did not choose, the actor counts the bodies behind him, and as he does so, he touches each of us. Again, we are cast – made part of his attempt to stabilize his count. Standing there as they decide who will be our Hamlet, we are made aware of, made complicit in, this always already failure of language and meaning to hold still.

This production of *Hamlet* did not sit still. From the dog on, the audience had to reorder the scenes and also hold characters attached to actors, even when they switched parts or when the other two potential Hamlets seemed to ghost the actor selected by us this night. The director, though, prepared us for this involvement in meaning by casting us as casting directors and by making us use our bodies as extensions of our voice/vote. We were not ever independent from the meaning of this *Hamlet*, putting it together involved accessing all these elements of the evening's performance; it required us to shake loose our assumptions that we know what it means to make meaning. This, I believe, is how the production – along with lots of other contemporary theatrical productions – is helping us to think differently. This *Hamlet* is not about the main character's internal psychology – his Freudian feelings for his mother, for example. This *Hamlet* is not about the possibilities of individualism in a growing modern world. It's not about the power of God to right the rot of the country – the providence of the fall of a sparrow. It feels like it's about the power of the group to stabilize temporary meanings. This *Hamlet* reminds me that characters can be cast and recast. It gives me a tool to imagine a world without a stable self or clear cause and effect. It calls my attention to my body, to a refusal to tell a clear story or to reward psychological readings. It is theater that I may not understand, in a traditional way, but it gives me a way to understand a new way of thinking about the world around me. It is theater I can use.

I am not arguing that the director of *The Rehearsal* engaged the spectators in the casting of *Hamlet* in order to facilitate or to stage alternate ideas about cognition. I am arguing that perhaps that is part of the effect. To think about how we might find our way from our bodies' movements to conceptions of cognition, I returned to research on gestures. The relationship between gesture and performance is older than Hamlet's directorial notes to the actor to "not saw the air too much with your hand" (3.2.3), older than Roman rhetorician Quintilian. Research on language and gesture in the last fifty years has shown that gesture coexists with speech. We think and speak with our bodies and hands. We do not just do this to perform or enlarge the impact of what we are saying; we gesture while on the phone, blind people gesture, and we gesture even when we aren't aware of it. A student comes into my office, puts her bag on one chair, and sits in the other. When the subject changes to the paper she is working on for my class, she nods toward her bag, saying, "I've made some progress, but it's not ready." The paper is not in the bag – it's not even the right kind of bag to contain a laptop or work folders, but I know immediately that she is gesturing to the bag as a stand-in for the paper – or rather, a stand-in for the bag that will someday soon contain the paper that she will bring to me. Later, when she references this theoretical paper, her gesture is compressed further to a glance, meant to remind both of us of what she's talking about. Gesture research exposes the potential of a shift to cognitive approaches to performance, as it demonstrates what we learn when we understand meaning as something performed, rather than conveyed.

Susan Goldin-Meadow and colleagues have demonstrated the role gestures can play in learning. While studying the gestures made by children who were asked questions about conservation and equivalence, she noticed some students expressed one set of explanations with their words but that their gestures suggested an alternate explanation. For example, some children were shown two glasses of water with the same amount of water – one glass short and wide and another tall and thin. They were asked which glass contained more water. The level of water on the taller cup was higher, of course, and many children pointed to the taller glass. When asked to explain, they either matched their gesture to their explanation, pointing to the height of the water while saying that the tall glass contained more water, or there was a mismatch between speech and gesture, indicating the width of the shorter glass but saying the taller one had more water. This same mismatch could be found when children were shown two rows of checkers lined up on the table, one spread apart more than the other, and asked which row had more checkers. Some children would say that the wider row contained more checkers, but they would gesture as if to match checker to checker along the row. Despite what they were saying, their hands were indicating the solution to the puzzle. Goldin-Meadow hypothesized that "[c]hildren who produce many gesture-speech mismatches when explaining a task are likely to benefit from an instruction on that task – reliably more likely than children who produce few mismatches. Mismatch marks a child as being open to instruction, and thus on the precipice of learning" (2003,

39–40). Our bodies, invited into the problem-solving situation, can help us find the way.

The fact that it is useful is because thinking is not something we do, algorithmically, in our brains. Thinking requires a body in the world. I continually rehearse and repeat my arguments for embodied and distributed cognition because I do not yet believe we have exhausted the opportunities for rethinking the arts and humanities based on a central role for the body and environment. As Rhonda Blair and I wrote in the introduction for *Theatre, Cognition, and Performance*:

> Embodied cognition is not something that requires explicit
> physical movement or action; cognition is embodied when
> we add up receipts, get a glass of water for a thirsty friend or
> reach for the shampoo in the shower. To say that cognition
> is embodied is to say that what we have called "thinking"
> requires the body and happens as it does because of the body
> we have. The problem is not with making our thinking or
> our performing more "embodied" – thought is always
> embodied. (Cook & Blair, 2016: 3)

When I reach for the shampoo, I adjust the speed and size of my gesture to match the size of the shower. My hand gets into the right shape to pick up the bottle and adjusts if the weight of the bottle is heavier or lighter than anticipated. Just because I'm not aware of this as a cognitive task doesn't mean that it isn't, in part, a cognitive task. If I were suddenly not able to do this, I would be seriously disadvantaged in our world. We take advantage of the embodiment of cognition when we use our fingers to count, gesture, or "mark" the choreography in dance.[21] The state of the body is not only an input into language interpretation; it is also an output. When we read "she handed me back the letter," we are much quicker to move our hands toward our bodies than away, for example, suggesting that the comprehension of the sentence accessed the motor cortex sufficiently to prime one physical

---

[21] See work by Goldin-Meadow (2003), Marghetis, Núñez, & Bergen (2014), McNeill (2005), Warburton et al. (2013), and Noë (2015).

action (movement toward) rather than another (movement away; Bergen, 2012: 79–80). Involving the body in spectatorship might also prime us to understand ideas about embodied and distributed cognition.

4.2 Personation, Creating, and Undoing the Self

We have always, I believe, used art and theater as a tool to think anew. The first person to cast a role was also the first actor. Thespis, the first person, according to Western theater history lore at least, to step forward from the chorus and take on the words of another, casting himself as someone other than himself. I think about this moment as the invention of a way of thinking about the self and other: I can stand in for Clytemnestra, and we can spin a story on a stage about revenge and think with and through our stand-ins. I see the beginnings of personation in church services the same way: a new tool to think with. When the Easter service included the Quem Quaeritis and the Marys and the angels dialogued about Jesus's resurrection, the story of Jesus rising from the grave allows us to see a chorus capable of "playing" Marys and angels. This enables a kind of thinking about our thinking, seeing ourselves as this and not that, and understanding the miracle of a far-off land and time as something that is happening here and now. During this same time period in Western Europe, farmers first harnessed horses for use on the farm. This isn't difficult to see as a profound technological advance: imagine what you can do, faster, when you add the strength of a horse to fieldwork. Someone had to have the idea first, but once the tool was created, it spread because it was useful. As Walter Ong (1982) argued about the effects that writing has had on humans, new technologies, new ways of seeing and doing, invite – demand – changing our minds.[22] Matt Hayler points out how "[t]echnologies . . . don't just allow us to do new things, they enable us to see new things, and to become new things – we are not human without our tools, and our tools seem to always be changing, as do we" (Hayler, 2016, 159). The Quem Quaeritis provided a new cognitive tool, and such is also the nature of casting that radically reimagines the individual.[23]

---

[22] Walter Ong, *Orality and Literacy* (1982).

[23] I explore this idea in more depth in "Staging Cognition: How Contemporary Performance Shows Us How We Think," in *The Cambridge Companion to*

One production, Forced Entertainment's *Complete Works* invites spectators to reimagine the individual, the self, foregrounding casting by separating the storyteller from the characters. The story is told using objects to stand in for characters; the director refers to it as a kind of "lo-fi puppetry" (Etchells, 2015). The actor tells the story while moving the pieces around the table.[24] Hamlet is "played" by a slender black bottle and is placed on a table to speak to the small juice glasses cast as the players. Each play begins with an actor sitting at an empty table. As he introduces characters in the story, he brings up an object from shelves next to him: salt shaker, empty ketchup bottle, and so forth. Behind the actor to the left and right are two industrial-size shelves with the "casts" of all the other plays to be performed over the course of the evening or festival.[25] One might think that a linseed oil bottle would be an inadequate Macbeth, but that would be wrong. Richard Lowdon, one of the actors, says in an interview with *Exberliner* magazine: "We're taking these plays, which are well-known and fantastically narratively driven, and we're making you actually care about the pepper pot or the salt cellar or the tube of glue. You're investing in these rather stupid objects" (Jacobson, 2015). As reviewer Laura Collins-Hughes noted in the *New York Times*, "Attended by handmaidens who were brightly colored spools of thread, Cleopatra was a filigreed creamer, her Antony a stoppered cruet – and it was somehow no less moving when they died at the end" (Collins-Hughes, 2018). Director Tim Etchells told *Shakespeare* magazine that "[i]t is initially a rather unpromising premise" but that "[t]here's something about how you handle the puppet, the attention you give it as a performer, that makes the watcher begin to invest in the objects as if they were characters" (Corley, 2016: 52). The writer for *Shakespeare* magazine invested quite specifically: "For some objects, labels

Theatre and Science, ed. Kirsten E. Shepherd-Barr (Cambridge: Cambridge University Press, 2020).

[24] I highly recommend viewing a piece of the performance here: www .forcedentertainment.com/projects/complete-works-table-top-shakespeare/.

[25] During the period of the festival, the performance was live streamed so, for those not in Berlin or London or Los Angeles, you could watch and tweet during the storytelling.

take the place of faces. In Lowdon's *Macbeth*, for instance, when Macduff (a can of kitchen sealant) booms 'Turn, hellhound!' and Macbeth (a half-empty bottle of linseed oil) swivels so their labels are facing each other, ready to duel, the atmosphere is electric" (Corley, 2016: 52). If we can invest in objects as if they are characters, might we think differently about our capacity for empathy? Or, perhaps more urgently, what counts as a self?

The impact of what Etchells calls "low-fi puppetry" is a reconsideration of where life begins and ends. As he says,

> Watching the objects arranged on the table for the end of *King Lear*, gathered around the body of *Cordelia* (as played by a small glass vial), Robin Arthur's glass vase representing Lear looking down to see if his daughter is still breathing; or watching Terry O'Connor's Richard II pontificate and philosophise endlessly, you're confronted in a double sense by the lifelessness of Cordelia, by the inertness of the king. It's the search for a speculative interiority that's compelling and baffling at the same time – the conundrum that's at the heart of puppetry, and perhaps, at the heart of acting itself. (Etchells, 2015)

Theatre history is filled with examples of powerful emotional reactions to puppets, from bunraku to *War Horse*. Just because we experience the linseed bottle as having emotions – or evoking them in us – does not mean that the emotions are inseparable from the character. We are feeling and thinking for the whole ecosystem. As I concluded in 2015, in response to my (and others') emotional reactions to the puppet horses in *War Horse*, "We are not precious as individuals with life, life is something spread out over the system, something that requires effort, labor, to generate and perceive. It is not a given and it is not isolated in the bounds of my body" (Cook, 2015: 534). Dispersed across the bottles and jars, the story comes across. Not the individual psychologies of the characters or the particularities of this world versus another world. What remains is an *idea* of storytelling. And if the objects can play their parts, perhaps we are too. Casting that counters a strong narrative about the individual, opens up a vision of the community, of who we are as connected neurons, rather than enclosed membranes. The metaphor we use to imagine shapes what we can see.

Steven Johnson's 2001 book *Emergence* argued that the metaphor of the twenty-first century will be the "swarm logic" of bees, ants, brains, and software – places where meaning and identity take shape from the actions of the whole: "Just like the clock maker metaphors of the Enlightenment, or the dialectical logic of the nineteenth century, the emergent worldview belongs to this moment in time, shaping our thought habits and coloring our perception of the world" (Johnson, 2001: 66). I started and ended *Building Character* (2018) with the image of the murmuration of starlings, individual birds that fly together creating a seeming whole, and I did so to invite us to think not about individuals but of a whole. The research on embodied and distributed cognition, as well as the crucial well-being of the planet and our species, call on us to challenge the science of the individual body, the individual self. Sometimes we need characters onstage to show us what that might look like.

5 The End of the Future

From *King Lear* to *Hamlet*, *Much Ado about Nothing* to *The Taming of the Shrew*, all the productions that I have seen between 2017 and 2020 have used casting in ways that used to be called "nontraditional" or "color-blind" but are now either conventional or innovative. It's not the actors selected in and of themselves that make the choice conventional or innovative – a female Hamlet, Lear, or Horatio is not inherently interesting – but the way the choice makes visible something previously difficult to perceive. Directors have always turned to Shakespeare to tell new stories – often radically changing the stories themselves in order to fit them to the needs of contemporary audiences. These days, directors are doing this through casting. By returning to characters we know well and staging them with a body we were not expecting, we can make a bridge from the past to the future. A male Lear is what an aging leader and patriarch looked like; now it looks like Glenda Jackson and Seana McKenna. Seeing a Shakespearean comedy with an all-black cast challenges the expectations white audience members have to see themselves everywhere and invites black audience members to see themselves love and laugh and sing and dance onstage in Central Park. To take part in the casting of Hamlet – to see three different versions of what Hamlet could look like and then actively take part in selecting your "flavor" of Hamlet for the evening – opens up a space between character and actor that challenges the stability of self. To feel for the tall dark bottle playing Hamlet – for what's Hamlet to him, or he to Hamlet – enables a vision of emotions and thoughts untethered to individuals, free to think about the ecosystem of the story, not the characters within it. In the bodies – and no bodies – selected to tell our stories, we can imagine a different future.

What I see, for example, in the work of Pan Pan and Forced Entertainment is a staged experience with distributed cognition. They take the stories and characters we know so well from Shakespeare, and they tell the story in such a way that we attend not to the individuals but to the group – not the Great Dane but Denmark. Distributed cognition is not a special kind of cognition, but rather a theory that counters a conception of cognition as contained in the brain. Although there are variations in how people define it, the term "distributed cognition" refers to the idea that what we think of as cognition is spread out of our brain, into the body, through the skin, and into the world around us. We find and create tools and we design workspaces in order to think with and through this body in this world at this time. Theories of distributed cognition insist on the situatedness of thinking, moving, and being, and are thus (in some ways at least) complementary to previous theoretical frames such as new historicism or cultural materialism. As Miranda Anderson has pointed out, the old saw about nature versus nurture, or the natural versus the cultural, is countered by a recognition of the inseparability of the body, the emotions, the mind, and the culture. Scholars always have deployed a theory of cognition onto our understanding of art, fiction, or the past; making that perspective explicit means we can challenge what we thought we saw. I agree with Anderson that "the study of cognitive phenomena cannot be considered a specialist niche, but is rather a necessary underpinning of any study of humans in the world" (Anderson, 2019: 15–16).

Theatre gives us new metaphors to think our way out of trouble. At this moment, we need a new story about who we are in relation to the planet and its other inhabitants. When people tried to elicit a reaction other than "America first" to the news of the Amazon burning, they described it as the "lungs of the world." While the Amazon burning might not seem to affect me directly, it is clear that the destruction of the world's "lungs" certainly will. Finding a way like this to recast separate things as united allows us to see ourselves differently: not nations bordered by walls, but different organs keeping a body alive. It also recasts my relationship with the earth, as my health and position are always dependent on the vital environmental systems on a global scale. Similarly, if I think about myself as extending into my community – as being a part of the story and a part of the storytelling – then more matters than just my story, my safety, my life. There is a species-saving value to challenging the story of my bounded, discrete self. This story is being told in theories of distributed cognition within philosophy and cognitive science. And this story is being told in innovative theater productions. Theater allows society a place to stage and reimagine categories like self, life, and death during moments when they are placed into flux.

References

Anderson, M., (2019). Distributed Cognition and the Humanities, In M. Anderson and M. Wheeler, eds. *Distributed Cognition in Medieval and Renaissance Culture*. Edinburgh: Edinburgh University Press, pp. 1–21.

Barnett, L. (2014). Out of Their Minds: The Actors' Guide to Playing King Lear. *The Guardian*, January 12. Available from www.theguardian.com /culture/2014/jan/12/actors-guide-king-lear-simon-russell-beale (accessed on February 29, 2020).

Bergen, B. (2012). *Louder than Words: The New Science about How the Mind Makes Meaning*. New York: Basic.

Berry, R. (2004). Shakespeare and Integrated Casting. *Contemporary Review*, 285, (1662), 35–39.

(1989). *On Directing Shakespeare: Interviews with Contemporary Directors*. London: Hamish Hamilton.

Billington, M. (2018). *Hamlet/As You Like It* Review – Michelle Terry's Double-Edged Globe Debut. *The Guardian*, May 18. Available from www .theguardian.com/stage/2018/may/18/hamlet-as-you-like-it-review-michelle-terry-globe-shakespeare (accessed February 29, 2020).

Blair, R. (1985). Shakespeare and the Feminist Actor. *Women & Performance: A Journal of Feminist Theory*, 2(2), 18–26.

Blair, R., and Cook, A., eds. (2016). *Theatre, Cognition, and Performance: Language, Bodies, Ecology*. New York: Methuen.

Bowie-Sell, D. (2018). Review: *The Two Noble Kinsmen* (Shakespeare's Globe). *WhatsOnStage*, 31 May 31. Available from www .whatsonstage.com/london-theater/reviews/the-two-noble-kinsmen -shakespeares-globe_46719.html (accessed February 29, 2020).

Brantley, B. (2020). Review: In *Hamlet*, Ruth Negga Rules as a Player Prince. *New York Times*, February 10. Available from www

.nytimes.com/2020/02/10/theater/hamlet-review-ruth-negga.html (accessed February 21, 2020).

Brown, M. (2020). Sir Ian McKellen to Play Hamlet in Age-Blind Show. *The Guardian*, June 25. www.theguardian.com/stage/2020/jun/26/sir-ian-mckellen-to-play-hamlet-in-age-blind-show (accessed June 25, 2020).

Bruno, C. (2019). Casting Disabled Actors: Taking Our Rightful Place Onstage? In Syler, C., and Banks, D., eds., *Casting a Movement: The Welcome Table Initiative*. New York: Routledge, pp. 83–87.

Brustein, R., and Wilson, A. (1996). Subsidized Separatism: Responses to "The Ground on Which I Stand." *American Theatre*, October 1. Available from www.americantheater.org/1996/10/01/subsidized-separatism-responses-to-the-ground-on-which-i-stand/ (accessed January 2, 2017).

Carlson, M. (2001). *The Haunted Stage: The Theatre as Memory Machine*. Ann Arbor: University of Michigan Press.

Carpenter, F. C. (2014). *Coloring Whiteness: Acts of Critique in Black Performance*. Ann Arbor: University of Michigan Press.

Catanese, B. W. (2011). *The Problem of the Color[blind]: Racial Transgression and the Politics of Black Performance*. Ann Arbor: University of Michigan Press.

Cavell, S. (2008). *Must We Mean What We Say?: A Book of Essays*. Cambridge: Cambridge University Press.

Cavendish, D. (2017a). Exit, Left: Is It Curtains for the Male Actor? *Stuff*, March 3. Available from www.stuff.co.nz/entertainment/stage-and-theater/89764586/exit-left-is-it-curtains-for-the-male-actor (accessed February 29, 2020).

(2017b). The Thought Police's Rush for Gender Equality on Stage Risks the Death of the Great Male Actor. *The Telegraph*, February 23. Available from www.telegraph.co.uk/theater/what-to-see/thought-polices-rush-gender-equality-stage-risks-death-great/ (accessed August 29, 2019).

Cole, S. G. (2018) Review: Seana McKenna's Riveting Lear Comes at the Right Time. *Now Toronto*, January 17. Available from https://now toronto.com/stage/theater/seana-mckenna-s-riveting-lear-comes-at -the-right-time/ (accessed January 25, 2018).

Collins-Hughes, L. (2018). Review: The Bard as Bedtime Story in "Table Top Shakespeare." *New York Times*, September 12. Available from www .nytimes.com/2018/09/12/theater/table-top-shakespeare-review.html? searchResultPosition=1 (accessed June 26, 2019).

Cook, A. (2015). Bodied Forth: A Cognitive Scientific Approach to Performance Analysis. In Graves, N. G., ed., *The Oxford Handbook of Dance and Theater*. Oxford: Oxford University Press, 523–544.

(2018). *Building Character: The Art and Science of Casting*. Ann Arbor: University of Michigan Press.

(2011). If: Lear's Feather and the Staging of Science. In Reynolds, B., and Cefalu, P., eds., *The Return to Theory in Early Modern English Studies: Tarrying with the Subjunctive*. New York: Palgrave Macmillan, pp. 48–68.

(2010). *Shakespearean Neuroplay: Reinvigorating the Study of Dramatic Texts and Performance through Cognitive Science*. New York: Palgrave Macmillan.

(2020). Staging Cognition: How Contemporary Performance Shows Us How We Think. In Shepherd-Barr, K., ed., *The Cambridge Companion to Theatre and Science*. Cambridge: Cambridge University Press, pp. 176–187.

(2006). Staging Nothing: *Hamlet* and Cognitive Science, *SubStance*, 35(2), 83–99.

Corley, L. (2016). Table Top Shakespeare: Think When We Talk of Jam Jars . . . . *Shakespeare* 10, 51–55. Available from https://issuu.com /shakespearemagazine/docs/shakespeare_magazine_10/51 (accessed February 29, 2020).

Cote, D. (2019). Shakespeare in the Park's "Much Ado about Nothing" Is the Best Party This Summer. *The Observer*, June 11. Available from https://observer.com/2019/06/shakespeare-in-the-park-much-ado-about-nothing-best-summer-party-review/ (accessed February 29, 2020).

Crane, M. T. (2014). *Losing Touch with Nature: Literature and the New Science in 16th-Century England*. Baltimore: Johns Hopkins University Press.

(2001). *Shakespeare's Brain: Reading with Cognitive Theory*. Princeton: Princeton University Press.

The Daily Show. (2019). Comedy Central, July 17.

Dawson, A. B. (1996). Performance and Participation: Desdemona, Foucault, and the Actor's Body. *Shakespeare*, *Theory*, *and Performance*. London and New York: Routledge, pp. 29–45.

Delgado-García, C. (2015). *Rethinking Character in Contemporary British Theatre*, Berlin: De Gruyter.

Diamond, E. (1988) Brechtian Theory/ Feminist Theory: Toward a Gestic Feminist Criticism, *TDR*, 32(1) (Spring, 1988), 82–94.

Dry, J. (2019) Scarlett Johansson Clarifies Bizarre Comments on 'Rub & Tug' Casting Controversy, *Indiewire*, July 14, 2019, https://www.indiewire.com/2019/07/scarlettjohansson-rub-tug-casting-controversy-transgender-lgbt-1202157835/ (accessedMarch 12, 2020).

Edinborough, C. (2016). *Theatrical Reality: Space*, *Embodiment and Empathy in Performance*, Bristol: Intellect.

Etchells, T. (2015). Table Top Shakespeare: Nowhere to Run, Nowhere to Hide. *Exeunt Magazine*, July 2. Available from http://exeuntmagazine.com/features/table-top-tim-etchells/ (accessed July 24, 2019).

Everett, L. (2018). The Two Noble Kinsmen, Shakespeare's Globe, London Review: Barrie Rutter's Production Is Delightfully Inventive and Blissfully Clear. *Independent*, May 31. Available from

www.independent.co.uk/arts-entertainment/theater-dance
/reviews/the-two-noble-kinsmen-review-shakespeares-globe-barrie
-rutter-eliza-carthy-a8377146.html (accessed February 29, 2020).

Ewing J., Boudette N. E., and Dooley, B. (2019). The Fiat-Renault Merger:
Pitfalls and Potential Profits. *New York Times*, May 29, B1.

Frank, A. (2019). Scarlett Johansson Defends Her Desire to Play Any
Person, Any Race, or 'Any Tree' She Wants. *Vox*, July 16. Available
from www.vox.com/culture/2019/7/16/20695075/scarlett-johansson
-casting-controversy-response-political-correctness (accessed March 1,
2020).

Fuchs, E. (2000). *The Death of Character: Perspectives on Theater after
Modernism*, Bloomington: Indiana University Press.

Galella, D. (2019). *America in the Round: Capital, Race, and Nation at
Washington D.C.'s Arena Stage*. Iowa City: University of Iowa
Press.

    (2018). "Being in the Room Where It Happens": Hamilton, Obama, and
    Nationalist Neoliberal Multicultural Inclusion. *Theatre Survey*, 59(3),
    363–385.

    (2015). Redefining America, Arena Stage, and Territory Folks in
    a Multiracial Oklahoma! *Theatre Journal*, 67(2), 213–233.

Garber, M. (1992). *Vested Interests: Cross-Dressing & Cultural Anxiety*,
New York: Routledge.

Giannotta, M. (2019). Inclusive 'Much Ado about Nothing' Makes
Shakespeare in the Park History. *AM New York*, May 21. Available
from www.amny.com/entertainment/shakespeare-in-the-park-1
.31356629 (accessed September 22, 2019).

Goldin-Meadow, S. (2003). *Hearing Gesture: How Our Hands Help Us
Think*. Cambridge: Harvard University Press.

Green, J. (2019). Review: In Central Park a Much Ado about Something
Big. *New York Times*, June 11. Available from www.nytimes.com/

2019/06/11/theater/review-in-central-park-a-much-ado-about-something-big.html (accessed September 22, 2019).

   (2018). Review: What's a Woman's Role? All of 'Em, 'Bernhardt/Hamlet' Argues. *New York Times*, September 25. Available from www.nytimes.com/2018/09/25/theater/bernhardt-hamlet-review.html (accessed February 29, 2020).

Green, J., and Brantly B. (2018). Review: There's a Dark, Golden Haze in This Reclaimed 'Oklahoma!' *New York Times*, October 7. Available from www.nytimes.com/2018/10/07/theater/oklahoma-review.html (accessed February 29, 2020).

Greenblatt, S. (2018). *Tyrant: Shakespeare on Politics*, New York: Norton.

Hart, C. (2018). Theatre Review: As You Like It and Hamlet, Shakespeare's Globe. *Sunday Times*, May 27. Available from www.thetimes.co.uk/article/theater-review-as-you-like-it-and-hamlet-shakespeare-s-globe-kcjpdkkvv (accessed February 29, 2020).

Hayler, M. (2016). Another Way of Looking: Reflexive Technologies and How They Change the World. In Blair, R., and Cook, A., eds., *Theatre, Performance and Cognition: Languages, Bodies and Ecologies*. London: Methuen, pp. 159–173.

Henderson, D. E. (1997). A Shrew for the Times. In Boose, L. E., and Burt, R., eds., *Shakespeare, the Movie: Popularizing the Plays on Film, TV and Video*. New York: Routledge, pp 148–167.

Herrera, B. E. (2017). "But Do We Have the Actors for That?" Some Principles of Practice for Staging Latinx Plays in a University Theatre Context. *Theatre Topics*, 27(1), 23–35.

   (2019). Nevertheless, Whiteness Persisted. In Syler, C., and Banks, D., eds., *Casting a Movement: The Welcome Table Initiative*. New York: Routledge, pp. 49–54.

Hodgdon, B. (1992). Katherina Bound; Or, Play(K)ating the Strictures of Everyday Life. *PMLA*, 107(3), 538–553.

Hutchins, E. (1995). *Cognition in the Wild*, Cambridge: MIT Press.

Jacobson, R. (2015). Putting Shakespeare on the Table. *Exberliner*, June 22. Available from www.exberliner.com/whats-on/stage/putting-shakespeare-on-the-table/ (accessed July 24, 2019).

Jenkins, H., ed. (1982). Notes. In Shakespeare, W., *Hamlet*. London: Bloomsbury Arden.

Johnson, S. (2001). *Emergence: The Connected Lives of Ants, Brains, Cities, and Software*. New York: Scribner.

Lamb, C. (1899). *The Life and Works of Charles Lamb: Poems, Plays & Miscellaneous Essays*. New York: Macmillan.

Lister, D. (2016). The Opening of Two Shakespeare Productions Signal a Considerable Leap Forward for Gender-Blind Casting. *Independent*, June 29. Available from www.independent.co.uk/arts-entertainment /theater-dance/the-opening-of-two-shakespeare-productions-signal -a-considerable-leap-forward-for-gender-blind-a7109181.html (accessed August 29, 2019).

Loomba, A. (2006). Forward. In Thompson, A., ed., *Colorblind Shakespeare: New Perspectives on Race and Performance*. New York: Routledge, pp. xiii–xvii.

Lukowski, A. (2018). "The Two Noble Kinsmen" Review. *Time Out*, May 30. Available from www.timeout.com/london/theater/the-two-noble-kinsmenreview (accessed February 29, 2020).

Kachka, B. (2018). Mary Gordon and Glenda Jackson Talk Poetry, Theater and the State of Feminism. *New York Times Style Magazine*, March 21. Available from www.nytimes.com/2018/03/21/t-magazine/art/ mary-gordon-glenda-jackson.html (accessed February 29, 2020).

Marghetis, T., Núñez, R., and Bergen, B. (2014). "Doing Arithmetic by Hand: Hand Movements during Exact Arithmetic Reveal Systematic, Dynamic Spatial Processing. *Quarterly Journal of Experimental Psychology*, 67(8), 1579–1596.

McKelvey, P. (2019) A Disabled Actor Prepares: Stanislavsky, Disability, and Work at the National Theatre Workshop of the Handicapped, *Theatre Journal*, 71(1), 69–89.

McHenry, J. (2019). Queen of Kings: Glenda Jackson Does King Lear on Broadway. *Vulture*, March 8. Available from www.vulture.com/2019/03/king-lear-glenda-jackson.html (accessed February 29, 2020).

McNeill, D. (2005). *Gesture and Thought*. Chicago: University of Chicago Press.

Menzer, P. (2013). Character Acting. In Karim-Cooper, F., and Stern, T., eds, *Shakespeare's Theatres and the Effects of Performance*. London: Bloomsbury Arden Shakespeare, pp. 141–169.

(2017). Performing King Lear: Gielgud to Russell Beale. (Writing Performative Shakespeare: New Forms for Performance Criticism). *Shakespeare Quarterly*, 68(2), 207–209.

Miller, G. (2014). Cross-Gender Casting as Feminist Interventions in the Staging of Early Modern Plays. *Journal of International Women's Studies*, 16(1), 4–17.

Mischo, J. B. (2002). The Screening of the Shrews: Teaching (against) Shakespeare's Author Function. In Starks, L., and Lehmann, C., eds., *The Reel Shakespeare*. London: Fairleigh Dickinson University Press, pp. 212–228.

Morrow, M. (2018). Review: Groundling's Fresh, Relevant Lear Speaks to Our Rapidly Changing World. *Globe and Mail*, January 15. Available from www.theglobeandmail.com/arts/theater-and-performance/theater-reviews/review-groundlings-fresh-relevant-lear-speaks-to-our-rapidly-changing-world/article37604433/ (accessed February 29, 2020).

Moschovakis, N. R. (2006). Topicality And Conceptual Blending: Titus Andronicus and The Case of William Hacket. *College Literature*, 33(1),127–150.

Nadarajah, N. (2016). Nadia Nadarajah: Sign Language in Theater Should Be Art, Not Access. *Limping Chicken*, June 15. Available from https://limpingchicken.com/2016/06/15/nadia-nadarajah-sign-language-in-theater-should-be-art-not-access/ (accessed February 29, 2020).

Noë, A. (2015). *Strange Tools: Art and Human Nature*, New York: Hill and Wang.

Ong, W. (1982). *Orality and Literacy: The Technologizing of the World*. London: Methuen.

Pao, A. C. (2010). *No Safe Spaces: Recasting Race, Ethnicity, and Nationality in American Theater*. Ann Arbor: University of Michigan Press.

Pye, V. C. (2019). Gender-Blind, Race-Blind, Ability-Blind Casting at Shakespeare's Globe. Presented at Shakespeare: Recent Innovations in Casting, Association for Theatre in Higher Education Conference, August 8.

Rackin, P. (1987). Androgyny, Mimesis, and the Marriage of the Boy Heroine on the English Renaissance Stage. *PMLA*, 102(1), 29–41.

Ranald, M. L. (1994). The Performance of Feminism in The Taming of the Shrew. *Theatre Research International*, 19(3), 214–225.

Rebellato, D. (2009). When We Talk of Horses: Or, What Do We See When We See a Play? *Performance Research* 14(1), 17–28.

Roach, J. (1993). *The Player's Passion: Studies in the Science of Acting*. Ann Arbor: University of Michigan Press.

Rogers, J. (2013). The Shakespearean Glass Ceiling: The State of Colorblind Casting in Contemporary British Theatre. *Shakespeare Bulletin*, 31(3), 405–430.

Rosch, E. (1998). Principles of Categorization. In Mather, G., Verstraten, F., and Anstis, S., eds., *The Motion after Effect*. Cambridge: MIT Press, pp. 251–270.

Rosenberg, M. (1992). *The Masks of Hamlet*. Newark: University of Delaware Press.

Royal Shakespeare Company. (2020). Key Moments and Facts. *RSC: Royal Shakespeare Company*. Available from www.rsc.org.uk/king-lear /about-the-play/key-moments-and-facts (accessed February 29, 2020).

Rutter, C. C. (2001). *Enter the Body: Women and Representation on Shakespeare's Stage*. London and New York: Routledge.

Sandahl, C. (2019). The Difference Disability Makes: Unique Considerations in Casting Performers with Disabilities. In Syler, C., and Banks, D., eds., *Casting a Movement: The Welcome Table Initiative*. New York: Routledge, 40–53.

Seymour, L. (2016). Doth Not Brutus Bootless Kneel? Kneeling, Cognition and Destructive Plasticity in Shakespeare's *Julius Caesar*. In Blare, R., and Cook, A., eds., *Theatre, Cognition, and Performance: Language, Bodies, Ecology*. New York: Methuen, pp. 40–53.

Shakespeare, W. (1998). *The First Quarto of Hamlet*, ed. Kathleen O. Irace. Cambridge: Cambridge University Press, 1998.

   (1973). *The Riverside Shakespeare*, ed. Evans G. B. Boston: Houghton Mifflin.

   (2016). *The New Oxford Shakespeare*, *The Complete Works: Modern Critical Edition*, eds. Taylor, G. and Egan, G. Oxford: Oxford Press.

Shapiro, J. (2015). *The Year of Lear: Shakespeare in 1606*, New York: Simon & Schuster.

Shenton, M. (2018). Review – The Two Noble Kinsmen at Shakespeare's Globe. *WhatsOnStage*, May 31. Available from www.whatsonstagec.om/london-theater/reviews/the-two-noble-kinsmen-shakespeares-globe_46719.html (accessed February 29, 2020).

Smith, B. (1999). *The Acoustic World of Early Modern England*. Chicago: University of Chicago Press.

Smith, K. (2018). Playing All the Angles. *The New Criterion*, 37(3). Available from https://newcriterion.com/issues/2018/11/playing-all-the-angles (accessed February 2, 2020).

Spolsky, E. (2015a). The Biology of Failure, the Forms of Rage, and the Equity of Revenge. In Zunshine, L., ed, *The Oxford Handbook of Cognitive Literary Studies*. New York: Oxford University Press, pp. 34–54.

    (2015b). *Contracts of Fiction: Cognition, Culture, Community*. New York: Oxford University Press.

Stern, T. (2004). *Making Shakespeare: From Stage to Page*. London: Routledge.

Strukus W. (2011). Mining the Gap: Physically Integrated Performance and Kinesthetic Empathy. *Journal of Dramatic Theory and Criticism*, 25(2), 89–105.

Syler, C. (2019). Introduction. In Syler, C., and Banks, D., eds., *Casting a Movement: The Welcome Table Initiative*. New York: Routledge.

Taylor, G. and Egan, G. (2016) *The New Oxford Shakespeare*, *The Complete Works: Modern Critical Edition*. Oxford: Oxford Press.

Thompson, A. (2010). "Ay, There's the Rub": Race and Performance Studies. In Werner, S., ed., *New Directions in Renaissance Drama and Performance Studies*. London: Palgrave Macmillan, pp. 178–194.

    (2019). The Chasm Between. In Syler, C., and Banks, D., eds., *Casting a Movement: The Welcome Table Initiative*. New York: Routledge, pp. 32–35.

Thompson, A., ed. (2006). *Colorblind Shakespeare: New Perspectives on Race and Performance*. New York: Routledge.

    (2011). *Passing Strange: Shakespeare, Race, and Contemporary America*. New York: Oxford University Press.

Thompson, E. (2007). *Mind in Life: Biology, Phenomenology, and the Sciences of Mind*. Cambridge: Harvard University Press.

Tribble, E. (2011). *Cognition in the Globe: Attention and Memory in Shakespeare's Theatre*. New York: Palgrave.

Trueman, Matt. (2017). U.K. Theater Review: Ian McKellen in 'King Lear.' *Variety*, October 2. Available from https://variety.com

/2017/legit/reviews/king-lear-review-ian-mckellen-1202577750/ (accessed February 29, 2020).

Vincentelli, E. (2019). Review: A "King Lear" in which You Feel for the Daughters. *New York Times*, April 12. Available from www .nytimes.com/2018/04/12/theater/king-lear-review-bam.html (accessed November 7, 2019).

Warburton, E. C., et al. (2013). The Cognitive Benefits of Movement Reduction: Evidence from Dance Marking. *Psychological Science*, 24(9), 1732–1739.

Warner, K. (2017) In the Time of Plastic Representation. *Film Quarterly* 71 (2) December 4. Available from https://filmquarterly.org/2017/12/ 04/in-the-time-of-plastic-representation/ (accessed June 15, 2020).

Wolf, M. (2018). Blind to Race, Gender and Disability, Shakespeare's Globe Goes a New Way. *New York Times*, May 31. Available from www.nytimes.com/2018/05/31/theater/shakespeares-globe-gender -race-disability-blind-casting.html (accessed January 30, 2020).

Ybarra, P. (2015). A Message from TAPS Chair, Dr. Patricia Ybarra. Brown University, December 4. Available from www.brown.edu/ academics/theater-arts-performance-studies/news/2015–12/mes sage-taps-chair-dr-patricia-ybarra (accessed November 29, 2019).

Cambridge Elements ≡

Shakespeare Performance

W. B. Worthen
Barnard College

W. B. Worthen is Alice Brady Pels Professor in the Arts, and Chair of the Theatre Department at Barnard College. He is also co-chair of the Ph.D. Program in Theatre at Columbia University, where he is Professor of English and Comparative Literature.

ABOUT THE SERIES

Shakespeare Performance is a dynamic collection in a field that is both always emerging and always evanescent. Responding to the global range of Shakespeare performance today, the series launches provocative, urgent criticism for researchers, graduate students and practitioners. Publishing scholarship with a direct bearing on the contemporary contexts of Shakespeare performance, it considers specific performances, material and social practices, ideological and cultural frameworks, emerging and significant artists and performance histories.

Cambridge Elements ☰

Shakespeare Performance

Printed in Great Britain
by Amazon